The Witches' Almanac

SPRING 2000 — SPRING 2001

For the first time combining the mysterious wiccan and arcane
secrets of an old England witch with one from New England

Prepared and edited by
ELIZABETH PEPPER and **JOHN WILCOCK**

CONTAINING pictorial and explicit delineations of the magical phases of
the Moon together with full and complete information about astrological
portents of the year to come and various aspects of occult knowledge
enabling all who read to improve their lives in the old manner.

The Witches' Almanac, Ltd.

Publishers   Newport

Address all inquiries and information to

THE WITCHES' ALMANAC, LTD.

P.O. Box 4067

Middletown, Rhode Island 02842

ISBN: 1-881098-10-9

ISSN: 1522-3183

First Printing January 2000

Printed in the United States of America

Preface

One of the world's greatest pleasures is seeking and finding. Whether it is the answer to an age-old riddle, true love, or a new world, the thrill of a quest lends life many of its finest moments.

Myth and history abound with tales of adventure and discovery. Trials, tribulations, a challenge met with honor, and the ultimate achievement of a desired goal define the glory of a quest. The themes belong to the human species and spirit as surely as does drawing breath.

Every one of us has a quest which perceived or not determines the very nature of our being. Only when we identify and detect its pattern are we able to control the creative process effectively. To vacillate, change course haphazardly, or veer wildly in several directions at once indicates that our internal compass may be temporarily out of order. At such times we are most vulnerable, and tend to allow circumstance and the opinion of others to shift us away from our primary goal.

And how do we recover and get back on track? The answer is deceptively simple. Follow your star, listen to your heart, and always pursue your dream. The effort a quest demands is valuable in and of itself.

HOLIDAYS

Spring 2000 to Spring 2001

March 20	Vernal Equinox
April 1	All Fools' Day
April 30	Beltane Eve
May 1	Roodmas
May 8	White Lotus Day
May 9, 11, 13	Lemuria
May 29	Oak Apple Day
June 5	Night of the Watchers
June 20	Midsummer Night
June 21	Summer Solstice
June 24	St. John's Day
July 31	Lughnassad Eve
August 1	Lammas
August 13	Diana's Day
August 29	Day of Thoth
September 23	Autumnal Equinox
October 31	Samhain Eve
November 1	Hallowmas
November 16	Hecate Night
December 17	Saturnalia
December 21	Winter Solstice
January 9	Feast of Janus
February 1	Oimelc Eve
February 2	Candlemas
March 1	Matronalia

CONTENTS

ELIZABETH PEPPER & JOHN WILCOCK
Executive Editors

KERRY CUDMORE
Managing Editor

JEAN MARIE WALSH
Associate Editor

Astrologer	Dikki-Jo Mullen
Climatologist	Tom C. Lang
Contributing Editor	Barbara Stacy
Consulting Editor	Margaret Adams
Production	Bendigo Associates
Sales	Ellen Lynch

Ultima Thule

With favoring winds o'er sunlit seas,
We sailed for the Hesperides,
The land where golden apples grow;
But that, ah! that was long ago.

How far, since then, the ocean streams
Have swept us from that land of dreams,
That land of fiction and of truth,
The lost Atlantis of our youth!

Whither, ah, whither? Are not these
The tempest-haunted Hebrides,
Where sea-gulls scream, and breakers roar,
And wreck and sea-weed line the shore?

Ultima Thule! Utmost Isle!
Here in thy harbors for a while
We lower our sails; a while we rest
From the unending, endless quest.

— Henry Wadsworth Longfellow

Ultima Thule — A phrase meaning a remote ideal or goal. In the 4th century B.C. the Greek mariner Pytheas discovered an island six days' sail north of Britain, now thought to have been Iceland. Pytheas named it Thule and ancient geographers used the name to designate the most northern reaches of the known world.

Memento mori Bamberg, 1463

If some persons died, and others did not die,
death would indeed be a terrible affliction.

— JEAN DE LA BRUYÈRE

MOON GARDENING

BY PHASE

Sow, transplant, bud and graft   *Plow, cultivate, weed and reap*

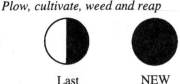

NEW	First Quarter	FULL	Last Quarter	NEW
Plant above-ground crops with outside seeds, flowering annuals.	Plant above-ground crops with inside seeds.		Plant root crops, bulbs, biennials, perennials.	Do not plant.

BY PLACE IN THE ZODIAC

Fruitful Signs

Cancer - Most favorable planting time for all leafy crops bearing fruit above ground. Prune to encourage growth in Cancer.

Scorpio - Second only to Cancer, a Scorpion Moon promises good germination and swift growth. In Scorpio, prune for bud development.

Pisces - Planting in the last of the Watery Triad is especially effective for root growth.

Taurus - The best time to plant root crops is when the Moon is in the sign of the Bull.

Capricorn - The Earthy Goat Moon promotes the growth of rhizomes, bulbs, roots, tubers and stalks. Prune now to strengthen branches.

Libra - Airy Libra may be the least beneficial of the Fruitful Signs, but is excellent for planting flowers and vines.

Barren Signs

Leo - Foremost of the Barren Signs, the Lion Moon is the best time to effectively destroy weeds and pests. Cultivate and till the soil.

Gemini - Harvest in the Airy Twins; gather herbs and roots. Reap when the Moon is in a sign of Air or Fire to assure best storage.

Virgo - Plow, cultivate, and control weeds and pests when the moon is in Virgo.

Sagittarius - Plow and cultivate the soil or harvest under the Archer Moon. Prune now to discourage growth.

Aquarius - This dry sign of Air is perfect for ground cultivation, reaping crops, gathering roots and herbs. It is a good time to destroy weeds and pests.

Aries - Cultivate, weed, and prune to lessen growth. Gather herbs and roots for storage.

Consult our Moon Calendar pages for phase and place in the zodiac circle. The Moon remains in a sign for about two-and-a-half days. Match your gardening activity to the day that follows the Moon's entry into that zodiac sign.

today and tomorrow

By Oliver Johnson

RAVE REVIEWS and major awards greeted Scottish author J.K. Rowling upon publication of her first novel, *Harry Potter and the Sorcerer's Stone*. Wonder of wonders, it soon became an international phenomenon. A book intended for young readers had crossed over to delight an adult audience. Two more books about Harry's adventures at a school for witchcraft followed with similar success, ranking one, two, and three on The New York Times Bestseller List for weeks on end. Harry Potter is well on his way to becoming a classic literary figure.

AFTER A GROUP of soldiers prayed to the goddess Freya and leaped over a fire at Fort Hood, Texas, the sparks began to fly. Republican Congressman Bob Barr said that allowing such ceremonies "sets a dangerous precedent that could easily result in all sorts of bizarre practices being supported by the military under the rubric of religions."

But the Army held its ground, noting that Wicca's *bona fides* are recognized in the chaplain's handbook, *Religious Requirements and Practices of Certain Selected Groups*. Even the staunchly conservative National Review chided Representative Barr by citing the heightened interest in witchcraft on television and in films. On the Internet, witchcraft features on more than 2,000 websites. The news magazine further states with some dismay, "It is generally estimated that there are around 50,000 Wiccans in the United States, a total that is said to be growing fast." May we expect the non-magical community to mount an offensive attack as the year progresses?

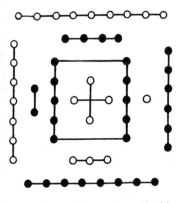

Ho-Tu, Chinese charm against evil spirits

BOWLS OF RICE and a scattering of pennies which kept appearing on the doorstep of a Chinese restaurant in the small Oregon town of Redmond indicated a developing feud which the local police chief described as "our version of the Chinatown gang wars." Reporting the story, The Wall Street Journal said that this was an example of how all across the country the casting of spells seemed to be on the rise. The article cited Arthur Wolf, a Stanford University China specialist, who said that the Redmond incidents appear to be a version of a generic Chinese curse, the paper stated. "Leaving any sort of offering on an enemy's back step does the trick," Wolf said. "It invites supernatural bandits and beggars instead of ancestors and friendly gods." The Redmond hexer was generally suspected of being the owner of a rival Chinese restaurant who resented her new neighbor.

IN THE PAST FEW YEARS hundreds of new *botanicas* catering to Santería worshippers have sprung up in Los Angeles. There are now more than a thousand such shops in L.A., more than in any other U.S. city. Santería, which developed among African slaves in 18th-century Cuba, is unlike other religions in that it is "very much attuned to solving problems in daily lives," explains Patrick Polk, archivist of the folklore and mythology program at UCLA. "It's the here and now. Can I find a lover? Where to find a job. How to cure this disease? It's possible solutions to immediate everyday problems, medical or spiritual."

A DISTINCTIVE African doll from Ghana with a large moon-shaped head and stick figure has been making its way into Western culture as a fertility symbol. The doll turns up frequently at African-American weddings in what The New York Times terms "this moment of millennial mysticism." The Ashanti doll, known as Akua'ba, is carved from porous wood blackened in oil, and has even been produced in soap. "I have had women call and ask for it (to be sent) Federal Express,"

Ashanti wooden fertility figure, Ghana

says Sarah Schwartz, who makes the soap figurines. "There have been pregnancies," she says significantly.

URBAN LEGENDS have become so ubiquitous that an Internet site specializes in checking them out. A recent list included such speculations as, *If the entire population of China jumped up and down at the same time, either the earth's orbit would be disturbed or the entire US would be swamped by a tidal wave* (false); *You can send a coconut through the mail without any further wrapping* (true); and *Koalas are always stoned/drunk from the alcohol in eucalyptus leaves* (false).

KING ARTHUR legends are so deeply embedded in our collective consciousness it's hard to remember there has never been evidence of his existence. Until last year. The British press went wild over the discovery of a 1,500-year-old piece of slate near a ruined Cornish castle that bore the name of the "once-and-future king." According to Dr. Geoffrey Wainwright, "This is where myth meets history. Tintagel has provided us with evidence of a court of the Arthurian period, with all the buildings, the high status archaeo-

Shield of Tintagel

logical finds and the name of a per son." The slate, measuring 8" by 14", i thought to be a plaque attached to building which collapsed in the 7t century. When another building arose on top of the previous structure the slate was used to cover a drain.

THE GROWING goddess movemen is spawning conferences and debate throughout the country, according to story in The Los Angeles Times. The paper reported a revival in the ancien deities such as the Roman Diana, the Egyptian Isis, the Indian Kali, and othe female deities. "Feminist spirituality is a hodgepodge of theologies, movements and motives," wrote Teresa Watanabe, the paper's religion writer "but the various strands are bound by conviction that women are as godly a men and must regain their rightful place of respect and leadership in the world' spiritual communities."

STONEHENGE WAS NEWS agai last year. Britain's Department of En vironment & Transport announced controversial plans for a new road t "rescue the stones from their squalid setting, wedged in the fork of a per petual traffic jam," as one observe described it. The trouble is, say oppo nents, that the new "cut and cover" tunnel requires digging a massive trench across the world-famous site and also will eliminate the inspiring

iew of the stones from the existing ighway. Archaeologists are outraged, elieving that the site will be desecrated y the new road, and Lord Kennet, resident of the Avebury Society, calls he plan "barbaric."

Meanwhile the English Druids were welcoming the restoration of their right o celebrate the summer solstice at Stonehenge after a 14-year ban. This unrise ceremony, the Druids say, had been celebrated by their predecessors or most of the 2,100 years since the tone circle was first completed by Stone Age astronomers. An unfortunate confrontation between law enforcement and enthusiastic visitors marred the celebration in 1999.

The giant stones that dominate Stonehenge are unique to a region of the Prescelly Mountains hundreds of miles away in Wales. After new dating ests proved that their arrival must have been thousands of years after the Ice Age, the BBC decided to examine the alternatives. Could primitive pagans have hauled the stones from their original habitat on sleds with rollers? They hired crews and devoted a program to demonstrating that it was possible. Of course, according to the 12th-century chronicler Geoffrey of Monmouth, the stones had been transported overnight by Merlin.

ANOTHER LARGE STONE hit the news in another part of the world. In Alexandria, divers led by a French archaeologist hauled up a giant sphinx with the head of Ptolemy XI. The pharaoh was Cleopatra's father, who died in 51 B.C. when she was 17. Oddly enough the plans are to return the massive sculpture to its place under the harbor with other objects that once adorned the city founded by Alexander the Great in 332 B.C. The director of Egypt's Supreme Council for Antiquities states that the organization planned to turn the whole site into an underwater museum by installing glass-walled viewing tunnels.

Cartouche of Cleopatra

BACK IN PRINT: *Magical and Mystical Sites,* by Elizabeth Pepper and John Wilcock. The treasured book has been reissued by Phanes Press, P.O. Box 6114, Grand Rapids, MI 49516. $16.95 plus $3.50 shipping.

ORION

He wheels across the heavens, Orion the Hunter, almost but never quite catching up to Taurus the Bull. Like the soldier, it is the hunter's destiny to slay, whether animal or mortal. And according to Greek mythology, so Orion fulfilled his fate before being dispatched skyward.

His story is interesting from birth. Two legends of his nativity come down to us, although one astonishing tale intrigues us by its very lack of details—he was born, according to some ancients, when three gods urinated on a bull hide buried deep in the earth. Otherwise Orion is simply known as the son of Poseidon. Like the other sea deity's children, the Hunter is gigantic and handsome. At birth, the father bestowed upon Orion the ability to walk on water, a gift of godly beauty.

Orion lived on the island of Chios, and a fire kindled in his heart for the exquisite Merope, daughter of the king He was spellbound by her flowing locks, her smooth cheeks, the redness of her lips, and he burned to possess her. But Merope, unmoved by his splendor, avoided him. Nonetheless, Orion begged King Oenopion for his daughter's hand.

Oenopion was the son of Dionysos and had inherited the god's tricky character. The king agreed to the marriage harboring a plan to dupe Orion. "We can have the wedding," he told the hunter, "only if you rid my kingdom of wild beasts."

Orion wielded his club and set to work—boars, panthers, lions, small furry squeakers, no creature was spared in his nuptial frenzy. The carcasses were laid in tribute at the silver-shod feet of Merope, who gazed at the gifts in horror. The more inert animals Orion piled up, the more she loathed him.

When the only creatures surviving were farm animals and tame deer, pets of the islanders, Orion approached the king and asked to set the wedding date. "Soon, soon," Oenopion assured him. Months passed and still the king remained vague. At last Orion realized that he had been deceived, and that "soon, soon" was the royal equivalent of never, never. He approached Merope and reminded her that he has labored mightily to rid the realm of wild animals and that the king had promised her hand in marriage. Again the handsome hunter sought Merope's love and pleaded with her to become his bride.

"Marry a savage like you? I would just as soon marry a wild bull," she told him icily.

Maddened by her scorn and he

12

ather's cunning, Orion took by force what he had hoped so long to be conferred. When Oenopion learned that his daughter had been ravished, his rage was boundless. He beseeched his godly father to punish the giant. Dionysos made Orion drunk, put out his eyes, and cast him out on the beach.

Blind Orion wandered alone and desolate until he heard the clanging of a hammer. Following the sound, he discovered the forge of Hephaestus. The smithy-god took pity on Orion's plight and gave him an apprentice, Kedalion, as a guide. Riding on the giant's shoulder, the youth led him on the long journey east to the abode of the sun god Helios, who restored Orion's eyesight with a beam.

With renewed vision, Orion's exploits with women continued and several stories account for his launch skyward. He became the companion of the archer-goddess Artemis, and together they spent long dappled days at chase in the forest. Their affinity inspired jealousy in her twin, Apollo, concerned for his sister's chastity. One day while Orion was striding underwater far from shore with just his bobbing head visible, Apollo pointed out the black speck on the horizon and maintained that Artemis couldn't shoot that far. The goddess drew her bow and knocked him dead with one fatal shot. When Orion's body rolled back to shore, Artemis bewailed him with many tears, although deities seldom cry. She atoned by placing him in the sky with a club, sword, lion's skin and belt of stars.

Another story maintains that Orion raped one of the chaste followers of Artemis, and the goddess avenged her huntress by sending a monstrous scorpion to sting the giant. And as Artemis placed Orion among the stars, she also thrust the scorpion into the sky. When the constellation Scorpio is just rising, still chasing Orion, the Hunter is just starting to disappear behind the western horizon.

But you may prefer the Pleiades account, the most fanciful tale. These were the seven daughters of Atlas, virgin companions of Artemis. Orion vigorously pursued them all, and the terrified sisters prayed for rescue from the lecherous giant. Zeus responded by changing them into doves and then into stars, where they still flee before Orion in the constellation Taurus. Six are pale, although visible, and Electra, the seventh, is said to hide her face so she might not behold the ruin of Troy, founded by her son. The poet Tennyson obviously miscounted the number of Pleiades, but in fine lines: "Many a night I saw the Pleiades, rising through the mellow shade, / Glitter like a swarm of fireflies tangled in a silver braid."

And so go the lovely Greek stories of the huge galactic chase, Scorpio pursuing Orion, relentless Orion still pursuing the shy Pleiades.

—BARBARA STACY

THE TWELVE HUNTSMEN

ONCE upon a time there was a King's son who was betrothed to a Princess whom he dearly loved. One day as he sat by her side feeling very happy, a messenger came from the Prince's father, who was lying ill, to summon him home as he wished to see him before he died. He said to his beloved, "Alas! I must go away and leave you now, but take this ring and wear it as a remembrance of me, and when I am King, I will return and fetch you away."

Then he rode off, and when he got home he found his father mortally ill and very near death. His father said, "My dear son, I have desired to see you again before my end. Promise me, I beg of you, that you will marry the bride I have chosen for you." And he then named the daughter of a neighboring King who he was anxious should be his son's wife. The Prince was so overwhelmed with grief that he could think of nothing but his father, and without reflecting promised to do what his father wished. Thereupon the King closed his eyes and died.

After the Prince had been proclaimed King, and the usual time of mourning was past, he felt that he must keep the promise he had made to his father. He sent to ask for the hand of the King's daughter, which was granted to him at once.

Now, his first love heard of this, and the thought of her lover's faithlessness grieved her so much that she pined away and nearly died. The King, her father, asked, "My dearest child, why are you so unhappy? If there is anything you wish for, say so, and you shall have it."

His daughter reflected for a moment, and then said, "Dear father, I wish for eleven maidens as nearly as possible of the same height, age, and appearance as myself." The King answered, "If the thing is possible your wish shall be fulfilled." Then he caused a search to be made all over his kingdom till eleven maidens were found, all exactly like his daughter. The princess ordered twelve huntsmen's suits to be made, which she commanded the maidens to wear, putting on the twelfth herself. After this she took leave of her father, and rode off with her girls to the court of her former lover. She asked him if he wanted any huntsmen, and whether he would take them all into his service. The King did not recognize her, but as they were all so handsome, he said, "Yes, I will gladly engage them." So they became the twelve royal huntsmen.

Now, the King had a most remarkable Lion, for it knew every hidden or secret thing. He said to the King one evening, "You fancy you have twelve huntsmen here, don't you?"

"Yes, certainly," said the King, "they are twelve huntsmen."

The King consults his Lion   H.J. Ford, 1892

"You are mistaken," said the Lion. "They are twelve maidens."

"That cannot possibly be," replied the King. "How do you mean to prove that?"

"Just have some peas strewn in your anteroom tomorrow, and you will soon see," said the Lion, "men have a strong, firm tread, and when they walk on peas, the peas don't move. But maidens trip, slip, and slide, and make the peas roll about." The King was pleased with the Lion's advice, and ordered the peas to be strewn on the floor of the anteroom. Fortunately one of the King's servants had become very partial to the young huntsmen, and hearing of the trial they were to be put to, he went to them and said, "The Lion wants to prove to the King that you are only girls." And he told them all the plot. The Princess thanked him for his help,

15

and after he was gone she said to her maidens, "Now make every effort to tread firmly on the peas."

Next morning, when the King sent for his twelve huntsmen, and they passed through the anteroom which was plentifully strewn with peas, they trod so firmly and walked with such a steady, strong step that not a single pea rolled away or even so much as stirred. After they were gone the King said to the Lion, "There now, you have been telling lies. You see yourself they walk like men."

"Because they knew they were being put to the test," answered the Lion, "and so they made an effort. Just have a dozen spinning wheels placed in the anteroom. When they pass through they will be delighted at the sight, as no man would be."

The King was pleased with the advice, and ordered twelve spinning wheels to be placed in the anteroom. But the kindly servant again warned the huntsmen of this fresh plot. Then, as soon as the King's daughter was alone with her maidens, she exclaimed: "Now, pray make a great effort and don't even look at the spinning wheels."

When the King sent for his twelve huntsmen next morning they walked through the anteroom without even casting a glance at the spinning wheels. Then the King said to the Lion, "You

have deceived me again. They are men for they never once looked at the spinning wheels." The Lion replied: "They knew that they were on trial and restrained themselves." But the King declined to believe the Lion any longer.

So the twelve huntsmen continued to follow the King, and he grew daily fonder of them. Now it happened one day when they were all out hunting that the news came of the royal bride's approach. When the true bride heard of this she felt as if a knife had pierced her heart, and she fell fainting to the ground. The King, fearing something had happened to his favorite huntsman, ran to help, and pulled off his gloves. Then he saw the ring which he had given his first love, and as he gazed into her face he knew her again, and his heart was so touched that he kissed her, and as she opened her eyes, he cried: "I am thine and thou art mine, and no power on earth can alter that."

To the other Princess he dispatched a messenger to beg her to return to her own kingdom with all speed. "For," said he, "I have got a wife, and he who finds an old key again does not require a new one." Thereupon the wedding was celebrated with great pomp, and the Lion was restored to royal favor, for after all, he had spoken the truth.

— THE BROTHERS GRIMM

Exploring
the
CANARIES

ISLES OF THE BLEST or FORTU-
NATE ISLANDS, placed in Greek
mythology in the Western ocean, and
peopled, not by the dead, but by mortals upon whom the gods had conferred immortality. Medieval map-
makers named the Canaries *Fortunatae
insulae.*

—ENCYCLOPEDIA BRITANNICA

F OR centuries the Canary Islands,
60 miles off the coast of Africa,
were an aspirant for the location of
Plato's Atlantis, described as lying west
of Gibralter. The claim has been dis-
counted only because the youngest of
the volcanic islands is over two million
years old, far too old to qualify for the
Atlantis myth. Another prevailing belief is that the islands were named for
the native yellow songbirds while just
the opposite is true. Pliny the Elder
dubbed the islands "Canaria," from the
Latin, *canis*: a dog, because of the
multitude of large and savage dogs
said to live there. Plutarch had a more
poetic image of the site, which he
termed "the Isles of the Blest."

The original inhabitants, the
Guanches, go back to the Stone Age
and lived in hewn caves with reed
ceilings. Anthropologists believe the
aborigines were of Iberian stock, and
closely allied to the Basques and the
Celts. They left no writing, only a kind
of pictograph script carved on rocks
and pottery which has never been deci-
phered. A curious whistling language,
unique in the world, survives to the
present day in remote mountainous
regions.

Gran Canaria, largest of the seven
islands, was ruled by two kings, the
guanartemes, one based in the western
capital of Galdar, the other at Telde.
All worshipped Acoran, the Greatest
or Highest, who required animal sacrifice. The rituals took place at cave
sanctuaries or on sacred mountains such
as Roque Bentaiga, which dominates
the center of the island. The monar-
chies were hereditary, and the societies maintained an aristocracy into

which people could be elected. The Fayan was the chief noble, male or female, and the office combined the roles of ruling judge and high priest. Women had an equal role in the culture and fought alongside men in battle. Adultery was not tolerated, and guilty lovers were buried alive.

Galdar is called, sometimes wistfully, by its medieval name, *Ciudad de los Guanartemes*, "City of the Rulers." The "rulers" refer to Tenesor Semidan and his Guanche predecessors, who governed the island from a palace now occupied by the site of a 19th-century Spanish church. In a secluded courtyard off the church square looms a gigantic dragon tree anciently revered by the Guanche. The tribe once conducted religious rites within its hollow "trunk," the space formed by twining branches creating an enclosure. Both trunk and branches are smooth and bare, sprouting no foliage except short spearlike leaves at the tips. When the wood is cut, it oozes a thick blood-red resin believed by Greeks, Romans and Arabs to have medicinal properties.

The most noted landmark in Galdar is the Painted Cave, the former haunt

Spanish galleon   Barcelona, 1439

of the virgin Andamana, who was reputedly a "mediator of great wisdom." The sacred spot is actually a series of seven caves, enigmatically decorated with geometric designs—triangles, squares, and black, white and red concentric circles. A replica of the Painted Cave is on display at the *Museo Canario* in Las Palmas.

The Spanish invaded the Canary Islands during the late 15th century, resulting in the usual historical bad news. Although the Guanches fought almost to the last man, by the end of the century they had been virtually exterminated. A poignant monument in the mountains commemorates their last hero, Doramas, slain by the lance of a Spanish soldier, whereupon Doramas' remaining followers threw themselves into the adjoining ravine.

Near Telde, Gran Canaria's second city, is the sacred mountain *Cuatro Puertas* (Four Doors), recognized at a distance by four square openings in a row just below the crest. Religious ceremonies are presumed to have taken place in the complex of caves, terraces, and platforms behind the four neatly cut doors.

This vicinity was the subject of a 16th-century report to the Spanish king from a military engineer who wrote that some 14,000 Guanche cave dwellings had been found there. Today, an easy walk from the village of Agüimes along a gravel track into the Barranco de Guayadeque demonstrates that caves are eternally useful. In Guanche times this was the most densely populated region and now many of their ancient cave homes are transformed into modern dwellings and even restaurants.

The engineer also reported that early Canarians "lived without knowing or feeling illness, at least until they reached the age of 120 or 140. Although their health may also in part be ascribed to the perfection and mildness of the air, yet the main reason must lie in the modest range of foodstuffs, none discordant with another, on which they lived—only barley, boiled, steamed or roast meat, milk and butter, all of which contribute to human health."

Three centuries after the Guanches had been defeated, the 18th-century Spanish historian Viera observed, apparently without irony, that although the conquest "almost led to the islanders' disappearance from the world, there's no doubt that this was more than compensated by the knowledge they gained of the true religion."

The colonial Spanish, secure in their arrogance, felt no need to destroy evidence of the former Canarian culture. Guanche relics—skulls, mummified bodies, homes, sacred places of worship, monuments—even descendants of the fierce dogs for whom the islands are named remain on one or another of the seven wind-swept isles. The relics may provide vital clues to understanding an ancient isolated culture, an intriguing mystery waiting to be solved. Perhaps part of the Atlantis myth to question is its overnight destruction and disappearance into the sea.

YEAR OF THE DRAGON
February 5, 2000 to January 23, 2001

The dragon is the only mythical creature in the Oriental zodiac. His attributes are strength, creativity, wisdom, and splendor. A benevolent being in the East, the Dragon is conceived as a scaly serpent, while the European equivalent is more lizardlike and winged. Both share an association with water and hidden places where treasure is concealed.

A Dragon Year promises riches, harmony, virtue, and growth. It seems entirely appropriate that our millennium should begin with such a pleasing portent of prosperity.

Eastern astrological years run in cycles of twelve, each under the dominion of a symbolic animal. If you were born on or after the New Moon in Aquarius in one of the following years of the Dragon, you can expect high energy, excitement, and success in all your endeavors.

1904   1916   1928   1940   1952   1964   1976   1988   2000

The MOON *Calendar*

 is divided into zodiac signs rather than the more familiar Gregorian calendar.

2000   **2001**

 Bear in mind that new projects should be initiated when the Moon is waxing (from dark to full); when the Moon is on the wane (from full to dark), it is a time for storing energy and the wise person waits.

Please note that Moons are listed by day of entry into each sign. Quarters are marked, but as rising and setting times vary from one region to another, it is advisable to check your local newspaper, library or planetarium.

The Moon's Place is computed for Eastern Standard Time.

THE WISE FOOL

The Fool, from the Rider pack created by A.E. Waite and drawn by Pamela Coleman Smith in 1910.

At first glance the Fool seems to be a symbol of our powerlessness over fate. But bearing in mind his ancient geneaology, beneath the Fool's apparent weakness we know he hides a secret strength: his fool's luck. He will bob up again. He will return to life. He will win at last. Moreover, the Fool has exchanged outward contrivance for inner power. He has turned his glance inwards and come to terms with the Night side of Nature within himself.

—PAUL HUSON
The Witches' Almanac, 1976

♈ aries   March 21- April 20

Mars   *Cardinal Sign of Fire*

s	m	τ	w	τ	ƒ	s
		Mar. 21 *Meet a new challenge* Libra	**22** *Wild birds sing*	**23** Scorpio	**24** *Go back in time*	**25** *View life from a hill* Sagittarius
26 *Till the soil*	**27** ◐	**28** *Be true to yourself* Capricorn	**29** *Soar with eagles*	**30** *Wear an amulet* Aquarius	**31** *Resist temptation*	April **1** All Fools' Day Pisces
2 Daylight Saving Time 2 a.m.	**3** *On to the next adventure*	**4** ● Aries	**5** WAXING Honor Cybele	**6** *Michelle Phillips born, 1944* Taurus	**7** Hilaria Day of Joy	**8** *Dream your future* Gemini
9 *Scry for an answer*	**10** *Planting time* Cancer	**11** ◑	**12** *Whistle up the green wind* Leo	**13**	**14** *Delight in paradox* Virgo	**15** *Henry James born, 1843*
16 *Walk by the sea*	**17** Libra	**18** seed moon	**19** WANING Scorpio	**20** *Lose not substance for shadow*		

23

THE HAWTHORN TREE

The hawthorn is a small tree seldom exceeding 15 feet in height. Its long thorns discourage grazing animals, protecting larger trees like oak and ash that grow up beneath the hawthorn and eventually supplant it. It also affords thorny shelter for birds and other wildlife that feast on its scarlet autumn berries. Although it grows well in most soils, the hawthorn prefers damp sandy earth for germination and is often a bird-sown tree. The bark is dark grey-brown and splits into a pattern of random squares with age. The flowers grow in clusters of white or palest pink and exude an unusual scent.

Hawthorn is so strongly associated with the Celtic May Eve festival that "may" is a folk name for it. Whitethorn is another name popular in Brittany, where the tree marks fairy trysting places. Sacred hawthorns guard wishing wells in Ireland, where shreds of clothing are hung on the thorns to symbolize a wish made. The Roman goddess Cardea, mistress of Janus who was keeper of the doors, had as her principal protective emblem a bough of hawthorn. "Her power is to open what is shut; to shut what is open."

Thorn trees are bewitched, according to old legends, and the hawthorn in particular caught the imagination of all Western Europe from earliest recorded time. In some cultures it served as a protection against lightning; in others it was thought to have purifying power. It was deemed the tree of chastity by the Old-Irish. Greek brides wore crowns of hawthorn blossoms in May, but Romans considered the month of May an inappropriate time to wed and the flowering hawthorn an ill omen, especially if brought inside the home. To the Turks, the hawthorn signified erotic desire. Mother Goose, in whose name so much of our folklore literature is preserved, yields a beauty secret:

The fair maid who, the first of May,
Goes to the fields at break of day,
And washes in dew from the
hawthorn tree,
Will ever after handsome be.

♉ taurus · April 21 – May 21

Venus · *Fixed Sign of Earth*

s	m	т	w	т	ғ	s
					Apr. **21** *Welcome a stranger* Sagittarius	**22** *Expect the improbable*
23 *Pay all debts*	**24** Capricorn	**25** *Refuse to force an issue*	**26** ◐ Aquarius	**27** *Shift a burden*	**28** Floralia	**29** *Uma Thurman born, 1970* Pisces
30 Roodmas Eve	May **1** BELTANE ❀ Aries	**2**	**3** *Withold judgement* Taurus	**4** ● 	**5** WAXING Gemini	**6** *Glory in love and spring*
7 *Renew psychic power*	**8** White Lotus Day Cancer	**9** Lemuria *Honor ancestors*	**10** ◑ Leo	**11** *Irving Berlin born, 1888*	**12** Virgo	**13** *Ward off evil*
14 Libra	**15** *Observe the heavens*	**16** Scorpio	**17** *Solve a puzzle*	**18** hare moon	**19** WANING Sagittarius	**20** *Shelter a lost creature*
21 *Drift with the tide* Capricorn						

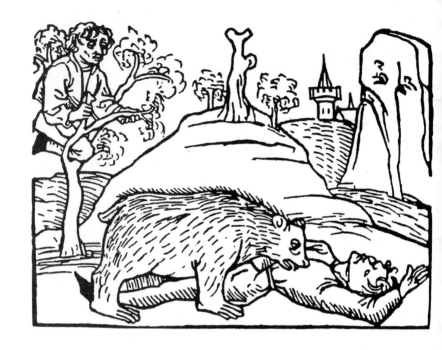

The Travelers and the Bear

TWO TRAVELERS were on the road together when they spied a bear. One made for a tree at the side of the road, and climbed up into the branches and hid there. The other, not so nimble as his companion, knew he could not defend himself all alone, so he fell down on the ground and pretended to be dead. The bear came up to him and sniffed his head and ears, but he kept perfectly still and held his breath. The bear, believing he was dead, went away. The other man came down from the tree and asked his friend what the bear had whispered in his ear. "The bear told me never again to travel with a friend who deserts you at the first sign of danger."

MORAL: Misfortune tests the sincerity of friendship.

From AESOP'S FABLES, literally translated from the Greek by George Fyler Townsend, London, 1890.

♊ gemini — May 22- June 21

Mercury   *Mutable Sign of Air*

S	M	T	W	T	F	S
	May **22** *Don the purple*	**23**	**24** *Explore an alternative* Aquarius	**25** *Avoid a blunder*	**26** ◐ Pisces	**27** *Isadora Duncan born, 1878*
28 *Eliminate the negative*	**29** Oak Apple Day Aries	**30** *Watch and wait*	**31** Taurus	June **1** *Mask your thoughts*	**2** ● Gemini	**3** WAXING
4 *Seek a clear horizon* Cancer	**5** Night of the Watchers	**6** Leo	**7** *Keep wits about you*	**8** ◑ Virgo	**9**	**10** *Plant herbs and vines* Libra
11 *Truth is elusive*	**12** Egon Schiele born, 1890	**13** Scorpio	**14** *Satisfy a longing*	**15** *Draw down the Moon* Sagittarius	**16** ○ dyad moon	**17** WANING
18 *Keep out of harm's way* Capricorn	**19** *Erase an error*	**20** *Resist greed* Aquarius	**21** SUMMER SOLSTICE			

The Evil Eye

For only last night, as they whispered, I brought
My own eyes to bear on her so, that I thought
Could I keep them one half minute fixed, she would fall
Shrivelled; she fell not; yet this does it all!

— ROBERT BROWNING

Renaissance Italy is the scene of Browning's poem. It tells of a young woman
rejected by her lover who visits an alchemist to procure poison to kill her rival.
Denied the power of the Evil Eye, she must resort to other means.

The Evil Eye is an age-old concept. The glittering, penetrating glance that can
wreak havoc has ever been a source of fear, and protection from its force a
universal concern. Innumerable incantations, talismans, and charms have been
devised to avert the Evil Eye. And how ancient and widespread is the belief that
certain individuals possess the ability to inflict harm with a baleful stare is clearly
revealed in many languages.

Arabia: *'ain al-hasad, 'ain al-Jamâl*
Armenia: *paterak*
China: *ok ngan, ok, sihi*
Corsica: *innocchiatura*
Denmark: *et ondt oje*
Egypt: *iri-t ban-t, sihu*
England: *evil eye*
Ethiopia: *âyenat*
France: *mauvais oeil, mauvais regard*
Germany: *übel ougen, böse Blick*
Greece: *baskanos*
Holland: *booze blik*

Hungary: *szemverés*
India: *ghoram caksuh*
Ireland: *droch-shuil, bad eye, ill eye*
Italy: *jettatura, oculi maligni, mal'
occhio, fascinatio*
Norway: *skjoertunge*
Persia: *aghashi*
Poland: *zte oko*
Scotland: *ill Ee*
Sardinia: *ogu malu*
Spain: *mal de ojo*
Syria: *'aina bîshâ*

cancer **June 22- July 23**

Moon   *Cardinal Sign of Water*

s	m	т	w	т	F	s
				June **22** *Carry a silver token*	**23** *Change is progress* Pisces	**24** St. John's Day
25 *Shun mediocrity* Aries	**26**	**27** *Mend your fences* Taurus	**28**	**29** *Check and verify* Gemini	**30** *Amanda Donohoe born, 1962*	July **1** Solar eclipse Cancer
2 WAXING	**3** *Dare to change your mind* Leo	**4** *Muggles galore*	**5** Virgo	**6** *Follow a fancy*	**7** *Haste is folly*	**8** Libra
9 *Collect sacred herbs*	**10** Scorpio	**11** *Delay all action*	**12** *Consider the source* Sagittarius	**13**	**14** *Maintain control*	**15** Capricorn
16 mead moon Lunar eclipse	**17** WANING Aquarius	**18** *Hunter S. Thompson born, 1939*	**19** *Full speed ahead*	**20** Pisces	**21** *Rise above trifles*	**22** Aries
23 *Music eases tension*						

29

ON MOUNT OLYMPUS

Every spring hikers congregate in the little town of Litohoro in northern Thessaly for an assault on Greece's highest climbing challenge, 10,000-foot Mount Olympus. It's a two-day effort for most people, and a couple of refuge huts near the top offer overnight stays.

Centuries ago the mountain was even more forbidding, for it was the legendary home of the gods according to the most ancient Greek writing—Homer's *Iliad*, believed to have been written more than a thousand years before Christ, and Hesiod's *Theogony* (800 B.C.). The mountain features in much of classical literature including the works of Pindar, Aeschylus, and Aristophanes. Olympus remained so sacred that it was not until 1913 that the peak was first scaled by a local climber, and in 1937 it was proclaimed a national park by the Greek government.

Covered with dense oak, beech, cedar, pine forests and abundant wildflowers, the mountain is now crisscrossed with hiking trails. Its snow-capped peak is rarely free of cloud cover, yet the heights of Mount Olympus often break through the misty shroud in a glowing splendor of sunlight. Homer wrote that the gods dwelled in cloudless *aither*, the pure upper air.

In that rarified atmosphere Zeus, the Sky God, reigned supreme over his divine family, an interesting mix of siblings and offspring. His brothers were Poseidon, God of the Sea, and Hades, God of the Underworld, both lower in rank. His sisters were Hestia, Demeter and Hera, the latter also his wife and mother of the only two sons legitimate by modern terms, Ares and Hephaestus. Aphrodite, Artemis and Athena were his daughters, and Hermes, Apollo and Dionysos his sons, all the result of chronic infidelities except for Athena, who sprang fully grown from the brain of Zeus.

The residents of Mount Olympus dined on ambrosia and nectar to the music of the pipes and lyre. They amused themselves by watching the activities of mortals on earth, cheering on their favorites and often joining the action by magical means.

At the foot of Mount Olympus, just north of Litohoro, is Dion, where Macedonians once gathered to worship Olympian gods. Alexander the Great paid tribute here before his final expedition in 336 B.C. A handsome mosaic-tiled floor depicts Dionysos, and the superb classical Greek plays are performed in the reconstructed theater at the site in August.

♌ leo — July 24- August 23

Sun · *Fixed Sign of Fire*

s	m	τ	w	τ	ƒ	s
	July **24** ◑	**25** Taurus	**26** *Gypsies celebrate this day*	**27** Gemini	**28** *Practice sorcery*	**29** *Mind over matter* Cancer
30 ● Solar eclipse	**31** WAXING Lughnassad Eve Leo	Aug. **1** LAMMAS	**2** Virgo	**3** *See how the wind blows*	**4** *Consult the Tarot* Libra	**5** *Halcyon days delight*
6 ◑ Scorpio	**7** *Mata Hari born, 1876*	**8**	**9** *Solve a mystery* Sagittarius	**10**	**11** *Music lessens stress* Capricorn	**12** *George Hamilton born, 1939*
13 DIANA'S DAY	**14** Aquarius	**15** ○ wort moon	**16** WANING Pisces	**17** *Harm hatch, harm catch*	**18** Aries	**19** *Gather herbs and roots*
20 *Obey an impulse* Taurus	**21** *Avert mischief*	**22** ◑ Gemini	**23** *Reap a random harvest*			

THE AMAZONS

A nation of famous women who lived near the river Thermodon in Cappadocia (modern Turkey). All their life was employed in wars and manly exercises. They never had any commerce with the other sex; but, only for the sake of propagation, they visited the inhabitants of the neighbouring country for a few days, and the male children which they brought forth were given to the fathers. The females were carefully educated with their mothers. They founded an extensive empire in Asia Minor, along the shores of the Euxine (Black Sea). They were defeated in a battle near the Thermodon by the Greeks; and some of them migrated beyond the Tanais (the river Don), and extended their territories as far as the Caspian sea. Themyscyra was the most capital of their towns; and Smyrna, Magnesia, Thyatira, and Ephesus, according to some authors, were built by them. Diodorus says that Penthesileia, one of their queens, came to the Trojan war on the side of Priam, and that she was killed by Achilles; and from that time the glory and character of the Amazons gradually decayed, and was totally forgotten. Diodorus mentions a nation of Amazons in Africa more ancient than those of Asia who flourished long before the Trojan war, and many of their actions have been attributed to those of Asia. It is said, that after they had subdued almost all Asia, they invaded Attica, and were conquered by Theseus. Their most famous actions were their expeditions against Priam, and afterwards the assistance they gave him during the Trojan war; and their invasion of Attica, to punish Theseus, who carried away Antiope, one of their queens. They were also conquered by Bellerophon and Hercules. Among their queens, Hippolyte, Antiope, Lampeto, Marpesia, are famous. Curtius (1st-century biographer of Alexander the Great) says that Thalestris, one of their queens, came to Alexander, whilst he was pursuing his conquests in Asia, for the sake of raising children from a man of such military reputation; and that, after she remained 13 days with him, she retired into her country. The Amazons were such expert archers, that, to denote the goodness of bow and quiver, it was usual to call it Amazonian.

—*A Classical Dictionary*
J. Lemprière, 1911

virgo | **August 24—September 23**

Mercury | *Mutable Sign of Earth*

s	m	т	w	т	ƒ	s
				Aug. **24** *Pay heed to censure*	**25** Cancer	**26** *Correct an error*
27 *Walk until weary* Leo	**28** *Take no chances*	**29** Day of Thoth Virgo	**30** WAXING	**31** *Observe the clouds* Libra	Sept. **1**	**2** *Hear no evil* Scorpio
3 *Collect five stones*	**4** *Search for an answer*	**5** Sagittarius	**6**	**7** *Patience pays off* Capricorn	**8** *Glory in life's gifts*	**9** *Gather fallen feathers*
10 *Enjoy a quiet day* Aquarius	**11** *Wakes Monday Horn Dance*	**12** Pisces	**13** barley moon	**14** WANING	**15** *Shift usual pattern* Aries	**16** *Carry an amulet*
17 *Elvira born, 1951* Taurus	**18**	**19** *Perform a candle spell* Gemini	**20**	**21** Cancer	**22** *Eric Stoltz born, 1961*	**23** Autumnal Equinox

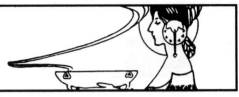

KITCHEN MAGIC

Certain foods and flavorings are touched with magic. Perhaps they are associated with old tales, spiritual significance, or simply a piquant taste that conveys something to us in an intuitive way. Whatever the reason, such feeling applies only to specific herbs and spices, fruits and vegetables. Other foods, delicious as they may be, don't inspire the same perception of mysterious properties.

Among the herbs, basil ranks high in mystical value. As any pesto lover can tell you, fresh basil, sharp and pungent, has a quality all its own. The herb teams beautifully with ripe tomatoes and fresh cheese for a simple, rustic Italian lunch dish.

Neapolitan Sandwiches

Add tomato slices to thick slices of Italian bread lightly brushed with virgin olive oil. Sprinkle with a splash of balsamic vinegar and cover with 1/4" thick slices of fresh mozzarella. Top with thin ribbons of basil leaves. Serve as open sandwiches.

Apple and Sweet Potato Crisp

The apple and the sweet potato, apart from their nutritional values, combine to create a mystic dish as satisfying to the spirit as to the tastebuds.

1/4 cup brown sugar
1/4 cup chopped pecans
1/2 teaspoon cinnamon
1 perfect red apple, peeled, cored, chopped
1 can (15.75 oz.) sweet potatoes
Miniature marshmallows (optional)

Combine sugar, nuts, and cinnamon in a bowl. Toss apple chunks in the mixture until well coated. Alternate layers of apple and drained sweet potatoes in 1-quart ovenproof casserole. Cover and bake in a 350-degree oven for 20 minutes. If desired, sprinkle with tiny marshmallows and bake uncovered 5 minutes longer, or until lightly browned.

Serves 2.

The Pomegranate

The pomegranate was a sacred fruit in ancient Persia, India, and the Orient long before the Greek tale was told of Persephone, Goddess of the Underworld. When the maiden was kidnapped by Hades and spirited below, she was tricked into eating some pomegranate seeds before being released to the outer world. The psychic power of the fruit secured for Hades his lover's eternal yearly return to the underworld.

Hundreds of red seeds, glistening like rubies and bursting with juice, are the edible portion of the pomegranate—the only fruit of which we eat only the seeds. With a sharp knife, slice away the stem end, quarter, and cut away the white rind for access to these tiny exotic delights.

libra	September 24- October 23

Venus   *Cardinal Sign of Air*

s	m	т	w	т	ƒ	s
Sept. **24** Clear the channels Leo	**25**	**26** Hear the message in the wind Virgo	**27** ●	**28** WAXING *Janeane Garofalo born, 1964* Libra	**29** Moon meets Venus	**30** Spend time alone Scorpio
Oct. **1** Collect oak leaves	**2** Sagittarius	**3** Erase fear with laughter	**4** Sing before breakfast	**5** ◑ Capricorn	**6**	**7** Do not bargain Aquarius
8 Seize the day	**9** John Lennon born, 1940	**10** Pisces	**11** Divine by candle flame	**12** Aries	**13** blood moon ○	**14** WANING Taurus
15 Define the limits	**16**	**17** Take proper precaution Gemini	**18**	**19** Delay decision Cancer	**20** ◐	**21** Protect your home Leo
22 Call the corners	**23** Wear an amulet Virgo					

A WELSH WITCH

After a fruitless search through folklore archives for a memorable witch of Wales, a 20th-century example turned up in an unexpected place — the autobiography of the Welsh-born film actor Ray Milland, *Wide-eyed in Babylon* (William Morrow & Co., 1974).

"Have you ever talked with a witch? Been fascinated and entranced by one? I have. Because in every Welsh village there is a witch. And people go to the witch for the fulfillment of strange and devious desires. For the Celtic mind in its lonely moments is a tumbling sea of love and compassion and romanticism and neurotic hates. I was born on a mountain called Cymla, above the town of Neath on the west coast of Wales....The name of our witch was Bronwen Madoc."

Milland describes his first visit to the witch when he was seven years old. He'd never done more than throw rocks at her cottage and run away with the other boys. It was dark, he was frightened, but he needed to know a truth and felt only Bron could supply it. He knocked, and a quiet voice said, "*Duwchymmer, bychan.*"

"She spoke only the Welsh tongue. I went in and saw her sitting on the hob, with a little black kettle whispering, ready for tea. She was old and in black, and she smelled of mushrooms and wet leaves. Before my courage died, I shouted to her, 'Bron, must I die?' She looked at me quietly and said, 'Death will come when you are ready for her.'" Milland fled, satisfied.

In true Celtic fashion, the actor recounts three visits to the witch. When he was fourteen he'd gone to beg a love potion, for he had found Gwyneth, the girl of his dreams. But Bron didn't smile, "Go home, *bychan*, and think only of me." Milland heeded her advice and his longing for Gwyneth faded.

Over forty years passed before Milland was to see Bron again. She seemed to have changed very little. She divined the reason for his visit before he realized it himself. "You want to know of Gwyneth, isn't it?" she said. She doubted if it was wise to rekindle a fire so long dead and Milland, reluctantly, came to know she was right.

Is there a witch in the town of Neath today? Did Bronwen Madoc pass on the secret doctrine to a young apprentice? It may well be so. Perhaps there is something in the human heart and soul that requires mystic nourishment. Witchcraft has satisfied that longing for centuries.

scorpio October 24-November 22

Pluto   *Fixed Sign of Water*

s	m	т	w	т	ƒ	s
		Oct. **24** *Kevin Kline born, 1947*	**25** *Julia Roberts born, 1967* Libra	**26** *Nature hates a vacuum*	**27** Scorpio	**28** WAXING
29 *Daylight Savings ends 2 a.m.*	**30** *Toss a token in the sea* Sagittarius	**31** Halloween	Nov. **1** HALLOW-MAS Samhain Capricorn	**2**	**3** *Evade a trap*	**4** Aquarius
5 *A loss is a gain*	**6** Pisces	**7** *Work and friendship are divine treasures*	**8**	**9** *Full speed ahead* Aries	**10** *Pay homage to the Moon*	**11** snow moon Taurus
12 WANING	**13** *Cherish a friend* Gemini	**14**	**15** *Bide your time* Cancer	**16** HECATE NIGHT	**17** *Trust your heart* Leo	**18**
19 *Hail the Elder* Virgo	**20**	**21** *Maintain poise* Libra	**22** *Leave well enough alone*			

HIGH JOHN
de Conquer

High John was a mythic hero during the years of African slavery in the Americas. Signifying a spirit of hope against all odds, High John brought courage and comfort to the beleaguered people. Zora Neale Hurston called him "our hope-bringer—the power and soul of our laughter and song," (*The Book of Negro Folklore*, Langston Hughes and Arna Bontemps, Dodd, Mead & Co., N.Y. 1958).

Hurston writes: "High John de Conquer came to be a man, and a mighty man at that. But he was not a natural man in the beginning. First off, he was a whisper, a will to hope, a wish to find something worthy of laughter and song. Then the whisper put on flesh. His footsteps sounded across the world in a low but musical rhythm as if the world he walked on was a singing drum." The old tales say High John returned to Africa when slavery ended, "but he left his power here," Hurston tells us, "and placed his American dwelling in the root of a certain plant. Only possess that root, and he can be summoned at any time."

The true root that bears his name is more than likely the sweet potato, a staple crop of the West Indies and our Southern states. It is the original potato, *Ipomoea batatus*, producing an edible root rich in starch and sugar. The plant's twining high-climbing vine adorned with violet or pale pink trumpet flowers attests to the virtue and quality of the godlike figure. The legendary root should not be confused with a Mexican medicinal root called "jalap," but marketed under the name of High John the Conqueror root. This odd case of mistaken identity would surely bring a chuckle from High John.

Today, those who practice conjure magic, and there are many, rely on High John's root as a last resort when all else fails to produce a successful outcome. Zora Neale Hurston remarked, "Thousands upon thousands ...do John reverence by getting the root of the plant in which he has taken up his secret dwelling, and 'dressing' it with perfume, and keeping it on their person, or in their houses in a secret place."

As an amulet, a sliver of High John the Conqueror root holds a subtle power to change bad luck to good and dismiss melancholy. Its virtue brings success in any situation, encourages clear thinking, and renews hope and courage.

Rock painting from Tsibab ravine, South West Africa

sagittarius November 23-December 21

Jupiter

Mutable Sign of Fire

s	m	τ	w	τ	ℱ	s
				Nov. **23** *A sly fox conspires*	**24** *Avoid a rough patch* Scorpio	**25** ⬤
26 WAXING Sagittarius	**27** *Words may not suffice*	**28** *See how the wind blows* Capricorn	**29**	**30** *Value is in worth, not number*	Dec.**1** *Weave a new pattern* Aquarius	**2** *A lie betrays itself*
3 ◗ Pisces	**4** *All things flow into form*	**5**	**6** *Find the still point* Aries	**7** *Maintain a steady pace*	**8** *Sinead O'Connor born, 1966* Taurus	**9** *John Malkovich born, 1953*
10 *Serve one another* Gemini	**11** oak moon	**12** WANING Cancer	**13**	**14** *There is but one of you in all of time* Leo	**15**	**16** *Silence has no pitfalls* Virgo
17 ◖ Saturnalia	**18** *Trust common sense*	**19** *Heed your inner voice* Libra	**20** Eve of Yule	**21** WINTER SOLSTICE Scorpio		

RUE
Herb of Grace

There's a strange, foreboding quality in the smell of rue akin to the sight of dark woods at twilight or the eerie moment of quiet before a storm breaks. The unique scent, somber blue-green beauty, and leaf form set rue apart from other herbs cherished by ancient Mediterranean societies, where rue acquired sacred significance. Its mystical association carried over to classical times, when it was believed that sprigs laid on the eyelids would bestow the gift of clairvoyance. To consume rue leaves promoted harmony between lovers, for the herb was said to increase a man's tenderness while it lessened a woman's anxiety. And the oil of rue was considered sovereign remedy against all manner of poison from aconite to bee sting.

The Romans introduced the plant to England during their nearly four centuries of occupation. There the herb became a garden favorite, in addition to its lovely color and magical reputation, because farmers found that a bank of rue near a barn discouraged flies and other biting insects. The herb's association with repentance only came about when its Latin name, *ruta,* was confused with an Anglo-Saxon word meaning "compassionate regret."

Rue was called the Herb of Grace in medieval times, an essential part of an herbal bouquet dipped in holy water and sprinkled over the congregation during the Roman Catholic mass. Rue, the purifier, was strewn over floors and carried as nosegays to prevent contagion during plagues. The herb never lost its mystical character as the Elizabethan poet Drayton reveals in his portrait of a witch: *Then sprinkles she the juice of rue / With nine drops of morning dew.*

A dictum of witchcraft asserts that amuletic herbs must not be purchased. A monetary transaction diminishes magical power. Several old herbals note that rue thrives best when the plant is stolen.

Ceremonial magic places rue under the dominion of the Sun, but Italian witchcraft's *cimaruta* (sprig of rue) is a silver charm honoring Diana, goddess of the Moon.

Naturalist Henry Beston said, "Were it ever to come to pass that I could have but two herbs in the garden, Rue would always be the other." In his classic *Herbs and the Earth* (Doubleday, Doran & Co., 1935), Beston pays tribute to rue as one of the ten great herbs: "Mysterious in colour and strange of leaf, potent, ancient, and dark, Rue is the herb of magic, the symbol of the earthly unknown, of the forces and wills behind the outer circumstance of nature, of natural law suddenly made subject to power."

capricorn — December 22 – January 20

Saturn   *Cardinal Sign of Earth*

S	M	T	W	T	F	S
					Dec. 22 *Stir the pot*	**23** *Humor eases stress* Sagittarius
24 *Determine your course*	**25** Solar eclipse Capricorn	**26** WAXING	**27** *Pleasure is variety*	**28** *The Sun is stronger* Aquarius	**29** *Mary Tyler Moore born, 1937*	**30** *Sharpen your wits*
31 *Burn the old year out* Pisces	**Jan. 1** 2001	**2** Aries	**3** *Ray Milland born, 1905*	**4** *Ride out the storm*	**5** *Try a bit harder* Taurus	**6** *Ingenuity solves a puzzle*
7 *Praise is in order* Gemini	**8** Janus Day	**9** wolf moon Lunar eclipse Cancer	**10** WANING	**11** *Hope invites success* Leo	**12**	**13** *A wish comes true* Virgo
14 *Happiness is activity*	**15** Libra	**16**	**17** *Claim your privacy* Scorpio	**18** *Life bestows gifts*	**19**	**20** *There is more time to enjoy* Sagittarius

OWL LIGHT

There was an old owl lived in an oak,
The more he heard the less he spoke;
The less he spoke, the more he heard,
O, if men were all like that wise bird!
— PUNCH, 1875

In Brittany to see an owl on the way to a harvest is considered an indication of a bountiful yield.

The ear openings of many owls are located asymmetrically, with one higher on the skull than the other, allowing them to accurately "fix" on the sound of their prey at night.

Australian aborigines believe owls represent the souls of women.

Crows are obsessed with owls and frequently chase them as social ritual. Follow crows to find owls.

In the Ozarks the call of a screech owl warns of sickness or approaching death. If an owl is heard near a cabin, a handful of salt is thrown into the hearth fire to silence the bird.

Owls lay pure white eggs.

In southern India the cries of owls are interpreted: one hoot is an omen of death; two predict success in impending endeavors; three foretell a woman entering the family by marriage; four warn of a disturbance; five prophesy travel; six predict guests will arrive soon; seven are a sign of mental distress; eight foretell death; nine promise good fortune.

Owls range in size from 5 to 30 inches.

Owls are associated with lightning in China. Owl effigies are placed in every corner of the house to protect against lightning strikes.

A young owl is called an owlet.

In Mexico the owl is considered the maker of the cold north wind.

Because their eyes are directed forward and are fixed in their orbits by a capsule of bone called the sclerotic ring, owls rely on the flexibility of their long necks to look in different directions.

The owl is known as consort to witches in many parts of the world, including Africa, Madagascar, and Sweden.

Owls are found everywhere except in the Antarctic region.

In Scotland it is considered bad luck to see an owl in daylight.

Twilight is referred to as owl light.

—KERRY CUDMORE

aquarius   January 21–February 19

Uranus   *Fixed Sign of Air*

s	m	T	W	T	F	s
Jan. 21 *A rare gift arrives*	**22** Capricorn	**23** *Fortuna Major*	**24** Year of the Snake Aquarius	**25** WAXING	**26** *Fate will guide you*	**27** *Mozart born, 1756* Pisces
28 *Colette born, 1873*	**29** *Observe the wild birds* Aries	**30**	**31** *Celebrate Brigit's promise*	**Feb. 1** Oimelc Eve Taurus	**2** CANDLE-MAS	**3** *Collect Sacred Water* Gemini
4 *Delay decisions till the 26th*	**5** Cancer	**6** *Find a key to unlock thought*	**7** Leo	**8** storm moon	**9** WANING Virgo	**10** *Heed a subtle warning*
11 *Raise the level of play* Libra	**12**	**13** *Maintain courage* Scorpio	**14**	**15** Lupercalia	**16** *Love is a random thing* Sagittarius	**17** *There is world enough and time*
18 *Enter a circle of mist* Capricorn	**19** *Sweep away doubt*					

Find Your Spot

Everyone entering a room for the first time generally pauses for a moment at the threshold before making a choice about where to sit. Should it be the blue easy chair or the hardback oak chair? The corner seat or the one in the center of the room? Maybe you would prefer to sit by the door to effect an inconspicuous exit if you intend to leave early. A witch, being a practitioner of sensitive arts, takes some subtle elements into account that might be worth consideration:

• Notice where animals are sitting, usually a good indication of pleasant energy.

• Avoid sitting near dying plants; they will drain your strength.

• Never place yourself between people who may be hostile to you. The psychic crossfire can be devastating and will probably cause a headache.

• Don't turn your back on the Sun or Moon shining through an open window. This is psychically rude.

• Try to sit by the side of a friend. The most subtle glances and motions can be extremely supportive.

• If you must sit close to a negative person, keep something between you — a vase of flowers or a table with bric-a-brac would do nicely.

• If someone is sending bad thoughts to you, try putting a pillow on your lap or crossing your arms to protect yourself from attack. If this fails, excuse yourself to wash your hands and third eye. Cool water will refresh your aura.

• If you are feeling uncomfortable or oppressed, seat yourself facing a window and frequently glance outside, focusing as distantly as possible. This will engender a feeling of freedom.

• If you expect to contribute to the conversation, place yourself in a good light. If you intend to be an observer, shadows are preferable.

• Sitting with your back to the door, especially a door on a north wall, is a poor spot, although this may not be negative in your own home.

• Avoid sitting in a corner. Psychic energy is drawn to corners, and you will feel as if you are sitting on a magnet. Your words will go unnoticed, so will you.

• A good conversationalist knows when to speak and when to listen. If you exercise that sensibility, you will find that people want to sit next to you!

— MICHAEL MARRA

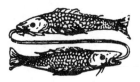

s	m	τ	w	τ	F	s
		Feb. **20** *Dream a new garden*	**21** Aquarius	**22** *Drew Barrymore born, 1975*	**23** ● Pisces	**24** WAXING
25 *Perform a candle spell*	**26** *Mercury goes direct* Aries	**27** *Resume action*	**28** Taurus	Mar. **1** Matronalia	**2** ◑ Gemini	**3** *Blackthorn winds blow*
4 *Rid life of needless burdens*	**5** Cancer	**6** *Waste no time*	**7** *Square all accounts* Leo	**8** *Think on your feet*	**9** chaste moon Virgo	**10** WANING
11 *Put your house in order* Libra	**12**	**13** *Reverse usual patterns* Scorpio	**14** *Protect your soul*	**15** Sagittarius	**16** ◐	**17** *Resist temptation* Capricorn
18 *Choose to be happy*	**19** *Bruce Willis born, 1955*	**20** *Perform a rite of spring* Aquarius				

45

ROMAN WIT AND WISDOM

His name may be unknown, but his words are recorded in virtually every collection of quotations. Publilius Syrus, a Syrian slave, was brought to Rome during the 1st century B.C., where his talents won the favor of his master, who freed and educated him. Syrus became an author of dramatic satires and achieved great popular success, crowned by recognition from Julius Caesar. He often acted in his own plays and was said to be without peer in the art of improvisation. All that survives of his work are extracts—one-line moral maxims, and Syrus is a master of the form.

A rolling stone gathers no moss.

It is better to learn late than never.

Every vice has its excuse ready.

Never find your delight in another's misfortune.

Everything ripe was once sour.

Frugality is wretchedness with a good name.

Money alone is the ruling principle of the world.

The loss that is not known is no loss.

Whom fortune wishes to destroy she first makes mad.

It is kindness not to excite hopes that must end in disappointment.

Friendship either finds or makes equals.

Ah, conscience doth make bondsmen of us all!

It is an ill plan that cannot be changed.

For the unlucky it is always best to do nothing.

Acquittal of the guilty damns the judge.

Pain of mind is far more severe than bodily pain.

What cannot be changed you should bear, not blame.

Practice is the best of all instructors.

He is not happy who does not think himself so.

No one can escape either death or love.

To take refuge with an inferior is self-betrayal.

Anger is one thing benefited by delay.

THREE WAYS TO BLESS A CHARM

E SSENTIALLY it is the quality of mind and imagination that can infuse an appropriate object with magical power. The ceremonial magician enhances consciousness by means of fasting, chastity, and cleanliness. The materials assembled for the ritual must be new. Timing of the operation, placement of planets, venue, and vestments are all vital considerations. Such elaborate preparations are believed to intensify the experience and secure a successful outcome. Or as witches say, "We will better when we're in the mood for willing." Three examples of typical blessing rites follow.

— From *Magic Charms from A to Z*

Blessing Ceremony   Greek, 470 B.C.

ANCIENT

One of the oldest texts describing a ceremony to bless an amulet is taken from a Greek magical papyrus written during the early centuries of the Common Era. The translation was published by the Cambridge Antiquarian Society of England in 1852 under the title of *Fragment of a Graeco-Egyptian Work upon Magic*. It has been slightly edited for clarity:

Ceremony of the Beetle

The scarab shall be carved out of a precious emerald; bore it and pass a gold wire through it, and beneath the beetle carve the holy Isis, and having consecrated it as written below, use it. The proper days of the consecration are the 7th, 9th, 10th, 12th, 14th, 16th, 21st, 24th, and 25th, from the beginning of the month of Thoth (29 August); on other days abstain.

Take the sculptured beetle and place it on a paper tablet, and under the tablet there shall be a pure linen cloth; under it put some olive wood, and set on the middle of the tablet a small censer wherein myrrh and kyphi (see note)

48

shall be offered. And have at hand a small vessel of chrysolite into which ointment of lilies, or myrrh, or cinnamon, shall be put, and take the scarab and lay it in the ointment, having first made it pure and clean, and offer it up in the smoke of the censer. Leave the amulet in the chrysolite vessel for three days.

At the celebration let there lie near at hand some pure loaves, and such fruit as are in season, and having made another offering upon vine sticks, take the scarab out of the ointment, and anoint thyself with the unction from it. Thou shalt anoint thyself early in the morning, and turning toward the east shalt pronounce these words:

Hail to thee, O Thoth,
inventor and founder of medicines and letters;
Come to me, thou that art under the earth,
rise up to me, thou great spirit.

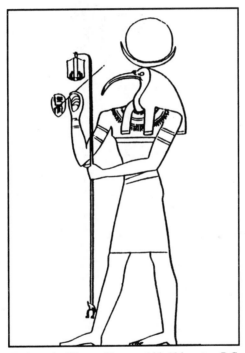

Thoth, tomb of Ramses II   14th-13th century B.C.

Note: Several arcane references may require explanation. Kyphi incense used in the ceremony was favored by the priesthood of ancient Egypt. According to later sources, kyphi consisted of juniper berries, myrrh gum, orris root, cardamom seeds, broom, sweet rush, honey, wine, raisins, frankincense and other resins.

Chrysolite is a volcanic green stone found throughout the world. Translucent or transparent, its color varies from yellow-green to deep olive and in its clear form provides the gemstones of peridot and olivine. Unction is another word for ointment or oil, especially used as a classical term for spiritual anointing.

Hans Sebald Beham, 1530

THE DOMAIN OF VENUS

MEDIEVAL

Ceremonial magic is a curious mix of archaic lore, astrological principles, Hebrew mysticism, and Roman Catholic rites. Rules of magic for spiritual work are contained in a series of *grimoires*, esoteric textbooks written in various European languages during the Middle Ages. The *Key of Solomon* may be the oldest, for a Greek version in manuscript form dates to the late 12th century. By the 16th century, the invention of printing spawned a succession of volumes devoted to ceremonial magic. To perform as simple an operation as blessing a talisman required extraordinary diligence. The following ritual is based on many themes culled from the medieval texts:

To Consecrate a Love Talisman

Love belongs to the domain of Venus, planet of poetry, music, joy, and harmony. That planet's placement was the first consideration. A well-aspected Venus should be in the zodiac's sign of Pisces, in direct motion, for a retrograde Venus would undermine the operation. The Sun must be in either Taurus or Libra, the signs ruled by Venus. The rite would take place on Friday, the day of Venus, and within the hours when that planet's power is strongest: midnight to 1 a.m., 7 to 8 a.m., 2 to 3 p.m., 9 to 10 p.m.

Early magical manuals decreed that the talisman chosen and all objects used to bless it must be new and never before used for any purpose. This strict rule extended to candles made from wax produced by bees for the first time. A simplification proposed by the *Grimorium Verum* (a French text dated 1517, but probably an 18th-century work) was a process of aspersion, an archaic term meaning to sprinkle with holy water, and fumigation. *True Black Magic* published in Rome in 1750 describes the instrument of aspersion: "And the aspergillum is a bouquet of vervain, periwinkle, sage, mint,

Venus pentacle from The Greater Key of Solomon, *16th-century manuscript*

valerian, ash, basil, and rosemary forming a brush. Fit it with a handle of virgin hazel, three palms in length, and dip it in a glazed earthen pot filled with fresh spring water. Sprinkle over all. This device may be used on any occasion with perfect assurance that all phantoms will be expelled from every place which shall be sprinkled thereby and so exorcised."

Fumigation was accomplished by "taking a new coal which has not been kindled, setting it alight, and while it is still black, exorcising it, saying: I exorcise thee, O creature of Fire, by Him Who hath made all things!" The fumes of incense placed on the live coal pleasantly dispersed any lingering evil spirits. A love talisman would be consecrated with scents most pleasing to Venus: aloes wood, ambergris, sandalwood, musk, rose, myrtle, and resins of galbanum and storax.

The talisman might be the symbol of Venus inscribed on parchment in black ink. A precious gem or a scrap of sea-glass engraved with an appropriate image must be green, the color of Venus. A square of duly incised and highly polished copper was another possibility, for copper is the metal associated with Venus.

The magician prepared with a period of fasting, chastity, and three hours of silence prior to the rite. A ritual bath and the donning of vestments followed. The 16th-century Italian *Grimoire of Honorius* advised a long surplice of white linen and bare feet as proper attire.

In a room reserved for magical work a sacred circle was defined by a nine-foot silk cord. Within the circle the purified objects were assembled: a small wooden table to serve as an altar covered by a white linen cloth, two white candles in glass holders, an incense burner to hold a fiery coal, incense, and the talisman. The candles were positioned to mark north on the left, south on the right, for the magician faced east in the performance of the rite. The room was darkened, candles lit, incense ignited, and the talisman was held aloft as prayers to Venus and her planetary angel Anael were recited. After the invocation, the magician asked that the talisman be blessed for his use and benefit. The talisman was left on the altar and not touched until the next day.

MODERN

Another way to bless a charm comes from a Book of Shadows kept by New England witch Katherine Irena Anderson during the early decades of the 20th century. While its practices are contemporary, they doubtless derive from ancient rituals handed down from generation to generation.

To Sanctify a Charm

While the Moon wanes, contrive to secretly burn a block of myrrh on a live coal. Sprinkle well with the dried crumbled herbs of rosemary and thyme.

Pass the object to be purified through the rising smoke of the incense until you feel it is quite free of any previous emanations. Wrap the charm in a square of pure linen and hide it away in a safe place.

At Dark-of-the-Moon and at the midnight hour, place the charm in the center of a triangle of white paper in a room lit only by a single white candle. Visualize a circle connecting the points of the triangle and concentrate with all the intensity at your command on the quality you wish to impart to the charm. Raise the candle and with it form a clockwise circle around the triangle three times. Take care to complete the final circle at the point where the first began. Stare fixedly at the charm. The moment will come when you will reach out and hold the amulet in your hand. Snuff out the candle and in the darkness feel the power of the spirit force brought into being. Address the charm with these words:

> *I greet thee, spirit, ye who dwell within.*
> *Be my shield against all evil and ill chance*
> *that may befall my body and soul in time to*
> *come. So be it. I place my sacred trust in thee.*

FOUR WINDS

When the wind sets from the east
The spirit of the wave is stirred.
It longs to rush past us westward
To the land over which the sun sets,
To the green sea, rough and wild.

When the wind sets from the north,
It urges the dark fierce waves,
Surging in strife against the wide sky,
Listening to the witching song.

When the wind sets from the west,
Over the salt sea of swift currents,
It longs to go past us eastward
To capture the Sun-Tree
In the wide, far-distant sea.

When the wind sets from the south,
Over the land of the Saxons of stout shields
And the wave strikes the isle of Scit,
It surges up to the top of Calad Net
With a leafy, grey-green cloak.

— From *Celtic Tree Magic*

Window on the Weather

The new millennium is an interesting time to evaluate the evolution of meteorology during the 20th century. We live in a time of rapid insight into the phenomena and cycles of constant change that shape long-term weather patterns impacting all our lives.

Through the ages, there have always been people with an innate concern for the impact of the weather on their settlements. During the Middle Ages, priests predicted the behavior of the elements. Their modern-day successors heading into the year 2000 ply their craft in the venues of universities, media outlets, and government agencies. Contemporary people involved in weather forecasting have the same immersion in the sensory aspects of weather, although they are now aided by radar, computers and satellite technology. As children, we fledgling meteorologists became enamored of seasonal changes that brought magnificent storms and times of tranquillity. All fascinated us equally.

Ending the 20th century, we now have a reasonable expectation of predicting long-term weather trends with notable accuracy. Vast meteorological data — measurements of heat, moisture, wind, and pressure — are instantly processed, transformed into predictions and made available to the public. Modern technologists are performing the same community service on a global level as their forebears effected on a tribal level.

Notable weather events of the past century are cited after each month.

— TOM C. LANG

SPRING

MARCH 2000 — The worst drought of the 20th century ends in the East. Rainy spells are frequent and long lasting from the eastern Great Lakes through New England and from the Appalachians to the Mid-Atlantic States. From Alabama to the Carolinas, squalls of thunder and heavy rain break from a generally overcast sky.

The Great Plains and frontal slope of the Rockies are drier than normal, with early season hot weather appearing in Texas and Oklahoma by the 15th.

On the West Coast storms cease, with the exception of the northern Oregon and Washington coasts. Several storms there will bring wind and rain to Portland and Seattle.

March 18, 1925 — A one-mile-wide tornado devastated all in its path from Missouri to southern Indiana.

APRIL 2000 — Coastal New England and the Mid-Atlantic States experience a dreary overcast and a wind-driven drizzle for a week or more. Temperatures are far below normal in those areas, while the Great Lakes States and Great Plains experience a stretch of beautiful spring weather.

Though rains are more sporadic in the Southeast, they will be intense and flooding can be expected in the southern Appalachians. Florida weather is exceptionally fine, as is the weather on the West Coast.

April 4, 1974 — The single greatest outbreak of tornadoes tore through much of the East from Louisiana to Ohio.

MAY 2000 — Wet weather will predominate in the East. Though no organized storm system will be apparent on the weather charts, abundant subtropical moisture will flow from the Gulf States through the Appalachians and into the Northeast. Rains will be especially heavy at higher elevations. Rainy spells will be mixed with intervals of sunshine lasting two or three days in the coastal cities from Boston to Washington, D.C.

Warm and dry weather persists for a third straight month in the Plains and Western Lakes regions.

In the West, the weather is sunny and cool with a pleasant Pacific breeze, interior valleys will experience temperatures often soaring to summertime levels.

May 26, 1989 — Temperatures soared to record high levels in the Southwest. Mercury hit 115 degrees in Phoenix, Arizona.

SUMMER

JUNE 2000 — The weather becomes stagnant throughout the eastern third of the country. Sunny intervals with invigorating polar air punch into the New England States. Several thunderstorm outbreaks precede a cold front's passage.

Days are murky and rain threatened in the Carolinas, particularly near the coast.

One notable tornado outbreak causes damage to northern Minnesota and Wisconsin; otherwise the tornado season ends farther south with less severe weather than in recent years.

Persistent dry weather threatens water shortage on the West Coast this summer.

June 15-26, 1972 — Hurricane Agnes swept over a vast area of the East, extending from Florida to Maine in one of the greatest natural disasters in U.S. history.

JULY 2000 — Last year's record heat will not be repeated in the East this summer. Instead normal warmth is accompanied by frequent outbreaks of thunderstorms which will cool what would otherwise be hot summer days. Mosquitoes and other outdoor pests will probably be more abundant this summer. In the year 2000, the country-side will turn lush and green throughout the East, in stark contrast to last year's desolate brown landscape.

The Central States will enjoy consistently fine vacation weather. Thunderstorms are confined to the U.S./Canadian border.

The West Coast is increasingly arid, with monsoonal rains flowing through the Continental Divide, providing abundant rainfall at higher elevations.

July 3, 1956 — The Northeast sweltered in record high heat. New York City suffered the highest temperature ever.

AUGUST 2000 — Rainfall eases throughout much of the East, though several episodes of intense rainfall can be expected with passing cold fronts. A fifth year of above-normal hurricane activity begins in the Atlantic Basin. The first major hurricane of the season forms in the Atlantic by the 20th. Rainfall is excessive from the Gulf States to coastal Georgia and the Carolinas.

Rain showers are sporadic in the Great Lakes, heaviest in the Upper Peninsula of Michigan.

Cooler than normal temperatures extend from the Eastern Seaboard to Wisconsin. Warmer then normal air is concentrated in the Great Plains.

Tranquil weather persists throughout the West.

August 17, 1988 — Chicago endured 46 days of over 90 degree heat culminating on the 17th, when record high temperatures were reported in as many as 55 cities.

AUTUMN

SEPTEMBER, 2000 — Four major hurricanes with winds exceeding 111 miles per hour or greater will intensify in the Atlantic and Caribbean this year. The risk remains high of a direct strike from New England to the Carolinas, with increasing strike possibilities also to Florida.

Elsewhere tropical moisture brings a return of some wet weather to the hill country of the Mid-Atlantic and New England states. Gusty southeast winds bring foggy nights to East Coast islands.

The West will be sunny and hot.

September 2, 1935 — The most intense hurricane in recorded history struck the Florida Keys with 200 miles-per-hour winds.

OCTOBER 2000 — In the East, colors change later this year after a summer of abundant rainfall. Fog lasts longer than usual in the predawn hours.

In Florida, a late-season hurricane hurtles west, skirting the Keys.

Midwestern states are dry and sunny and beautiful, enjoying abundant sun-shine and pleasantly cool nights. First frosts nip at the pastures of Minnesota, northern Wisconsin and Montana valleys.

Santa Ana winds are fierce in Southern California, exceeding hurricane force and spawning wildfires.

October 4, 1987 — An unusually early snowstorm blanketed Vermont and northern New York State with nearly two feet of snow.

NOVEMBER 2000 — The first East Coast storm forms quickly near the coast of Maine, blanketing the mountains of northern New England with an early-season snow cover. Icy air follows and streams south covering the remainder of the East Coast.

Early-season freezes can be anticipated in the Carolinas and Georgia. Crops may be threatened. Below zero cold for one day startles Midwesterners. Records are set by Thanksgiving. Lake-effect snows idle Buffalo, Rochester, and Cleveland. All Great Lakes cities paralyzed by local blizzards.

California is very dry and windy. Farther east, a nearly stationary storm system persists for weeks and brings cascading snowfalls to the rugged regions of Arizona and New Mexico.

November 25, 1950 — A fierce storm battered the entire East with winds up to 160 miles-per-hour and three-foot mountain snows.

WINTER

DECEMBER 2000 — Four major snowstorms will sweep through the East this winter, beginning in December. Powdery snows will be deep. Early-season snows will be confined to the eastern Ohio Valley through central and northern New England. A cold rainy night or two will be felt in the first week of December in the eastern coastal cities.

An icy blast from Canada jolts Great Lakes and Northern Plains residents as the solstice arrives.

The West Coast is brushed by a Pacific storm with little rainfall except in the higher elevations of the coastal ranges. The valleys continue to bake.

December 23, 1989 — A day that saw 41 cities report record low temperatures. Topeka, Kansas, hit 26 degrees below zero.

JANUARY 2001 – An icy cold snap early in the month is succeeded by a powerful, fast-moving blizzard barreling up the East Coast. Snow drifts are deep, with more than one foot of snow falling in 12 hours. This memorable storm will begin at sunrise and end by dusk.

In the Great Lake States, lake-effect snows usher in a brutally cold Arctic outbreak. Winds howl, averaging 40 miles-per-hour at the height of the onslaught. Wind chills plummet to 70 degrees below zero in the nation's heartland.

Though cold, western outdoor sports enthusiasts will relish fine conditions. The snow quality is exceptional, the air clear and dry.

January 22, 1989 — In Spearfish, South Dakota, the temperature rose from 4 degrees below zero to 45 degrees above in two minutes, a world record.

FEBRUARY 2001 — The month is highlighted by two formidable snowstorms that cover vast territories east of the Mississippi. The onslaught begins in the lower Ohio Valley with half-foot snows blanketing Cincinnati and Pittsburgh. The storm redevelops and snowfall becomes heavy from Philadelphia to Portland, Maine. The storm lasts for 36 hours.

Out west, a powerful storm crashes ashore from the Pacific and after bringing mud slides to Southern California, races east. Snows break out from Kansas City, Missouri, to St. Louis. The month ends with the immense storm buffeting the Northeast with heavy snow and fierce winds.

February 6, 1978 — All commerce was paralyzed for a week when the Great New England Blizzard buried the Northeast in record snowfall.

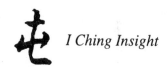 *I Ching Insight*

The I Ching or Book of Changes is an ancient Chinese method of divination. The querent formulates a question and tosses yarrow stalks or coins, the combination of which leads to one of 64 hexagrams. If your question involves a new enterprise and your toss leads you to Hexagram 3, its contents might offer insight:

CHUN
Difficulty at the Beginning

The Judgement
Difficulty at the Beginning works supreme success,
Furthering through perseverance.
Nothing should be undertaken.
It furthers one to appoint helpers.

The Image
Clouds and thunder:
The image of Difficulty at the Beginning.
Thus the superior man
Brings order out of confusion.

— *From* The I Ching or Book of Changes, *translated by Richard Wilhelm*
Bollingen Series XIX, Princeton University Press.

Chun or *Difficulty at the Beginning* is the third hexagram of the *I Ching*. The name is suggestive of a blade of grass pushing its way through the earth. The lower three-line trigram, *Chên*, is the Arousing. Its motion is upward and its image is thunder. The upper trigram, *K'an*, stands for the Abysmal, the dangerous. Its motion is downward and representational of rain. The combination of the two illustrates the chaos of beginnings.

If one waits patiently through the dangerous storm of chaos there is potential for success. Most will not. They will move obsessively into the storm and become disheartened with their quest. A premature move heralds disaster. But inertia is not indicated. It furthers one to appoint helpers while providing them guidance and inspiration.

Despite the chaos of the beginning, the storm provides energy that when organized and channelled wisely provides order. The clear air after the storm ulitimately reveals one's place in the infinity of being.

—KERRY CUDMORE

presage

by Dikki-Jo Mullen

ARIES 2000 — PISCES 2001

For hundreds of years prophets have hinted that special signs in the heavens would herald a new age with the year 2000. Looking at the star patterns for the coming year, one of the most intriguing of these will take place in July. There will be a highly unusual pattern of three eclipses, on the 1st, 16th, and 30th of the month. A time of new beginnings can be expected. All that has outlived its usefulness tends to be swept away to make room for new growth. There are elements of the unexpected, but the outcome is positive.

Your personal birth sign forecast will guide you through important turning points in the new year ahead so you can enjoy a bright future in every way. If you were born on the day of a sign change, called the cusp, both forecasts will apply. Check with your personal astrologer, who will use your place and

time of birth to ascertain which is your actual Sun sign. The Sun sign is the only part of the horoscope known to most people. It describes your ego, sense of purpose, and identity. The Sun sign forecast will reveal where and how your light shines. For more information, study the forecasts for your Moon and Ascendant or Rising signs. The Moon will offer insights about domestic and emotional needs while the Ascendant shows how you appear and function as part of the external physical world around you.

There's magic in the four elements: fire, earth, air, and water. Fire brings enthusiasm and passion, earth gives ground for a home and physical sensations, air is light, free, and spacious, water cools and refreshes. The signs of the zodiac contain them all, surrounding us with wonders.

ASTROLOGICAL KEYS

Signs of the Zodiac
Channels of Expression

ARIES: pioneer, leader, competitor
TAURUS: earthy, stable, practical
GEMINI: dual, lively, versatile
CANCER: protective, traditional
LEO: dramatic, flamboyant, warm
VIRGO: conscientious, analytical
LIBRA: refined, fair, sociable
SCORPIO: intense, secretive, ambitious
SAGITTARIUS: friendly, expansive
CAPRICORN: cautious, materialistic
AQUARIUS: inquisitive, unpredictable
PISCES: responsive, dependent, fanciful

Elements

FIRE: Aries, Leo, Sagittarius
EARTH: Taurus, Virgo, Capricorn
AIR: Gemini, Libra, Aquarius
WATER: Cancer, Scorpio, Pisces

Qualities

CARDINAL	FIXED	MUTABLE
Aries	Taurus	Gemini
Cancer	Leo	Virgo
Libra	Scorpio	Sagittarius
Capricorn	Aquarius	Pisces

CARDINAL signs mark the beginning of each new season — active.

FIXED signs represent the season at its height — steadfast.

MUTABLE signs herald a change of season — variable.

Celestial Bodies
Generating Energy of the Cosmos

Sun: birth sign, ego, identity
Moon: emotions, memories, personality
Mercury: communication, intellect, skills
Venus: love, pleasures, the fine arts
Mars: energy, challenges, sports
Jupiter: expansion, religion, happiness
Saturn: responsibility, maturity, realities
Uranus: originality, science, progress
Neptune: dreams, illusions, inspiration
Pluto: rebirth, renewal, resources

Glossary of Aspects

Conjunction: two planets within the same sign or less than 10 degrees apart, favorable or unfavorable according to the nature of the planets.

Sextile: a pleasant, harmonious aspect occurring when two planets are two signs or 60 degrees apart.

Square: a major negative effect resulting when planets are three signs from one another or 90 degrees apart.

Trine: planets four signs or 120 degrees apart, forming a positive and favorable influence.

Quincunx: a mildly negative aspect produced when planets are five signs or 150 degrees apart.

Opposition: a six sign or 180 degrees separation of planets generating positive or negative forces depending on the planets involved.

The Houses — *Twelve Areas of Life*

1st house: appearance, image, identity
2nd house: money, possessions, tools
3rd house: communications, siblings
4th house: family, domesticity, security
5th house: romance, creativity, children
6th house: daily routine, service, health
7th house: marriage, partnerships, union
8th house: passion, death, rebirth, soul
9th house: travel, philosophy, education
10th house: fame, achievement, mastery
11th house: goals, friends, high hopes
12th house: sacrifice, solitude, privacy

ECLIPSES

Since earliest times eclipses have awed stargazers. These mysterious temporary disappearances of the Sun and Moon were once thought to be caused by attacks from a gigantic sky dragon. The Moon's nodes correlate with the signs of eclipse activity. They were named long ago in honor of the head (north node) and tail (south node) of the dragon. North node eclipses are generally considered more favorable and south node eclipses more difficult. Eclipses promise excitement; they can herald unusual weather and world events which in turn will impact us as individuals.

There are five eclipses during the year ahead. If one should occur on or near your birthday anticipate a memorable year with great turning points. A new residence or a different relationship or career path would be highly likely.

July 1	New Moon Solar in Cancer with the north node–partial
July 16	Full Moon Lunar in Capricorn with the south node–total
July 30	New Moon Solar in Leo with the north node–partial
December 25	New Moon Solar in Capricorn with the south node–partial
January 9	Full Moon Lunar in Cancer with the north node–total

PLANETS IN RETROGRADE MOTION

Retrograde motion is the backward movement of a planet. Although this is really an optical illusion created by variance in rates of speed of travel between different planets in the solar system as we observe them, we do respond to it. Retrograde cycles bring a need to reconsider, revise, and rest. When retrograde, the planetary energies manifest in unexpected ways. They can be softer or blurred. Retrograde motion is not unfavorable, just different.

The most familiar and powerfully felt retrograde cycle is that of Mercury, which occurs three to four times yearly for about three weeks each time. While Mercury is retrograde, old patterns repeat. People from the past can suddenly reappear. Complete old business, but postpone moves or the signing of contracts. Get extra rest and verify appointments. Travel only to familiar destinations. It is an auspicious time for past life regression and ghost hunting. There will be three retrograde Mercury periods in the coming year.

MERCURY RETROGRADE

June 24–July 18
in Cancer

October 19–November 8
in Scorpio

February 4–February 26
in Aquarius and Pisces

As you study your own forecast in Presage, other planetary retrogrades will be mentioned when they impact your own birth sign. Activities ruled by those planets demand patience and revision. Karmic situations can be involved. For example, in the case of Venus retrograde a complex love situation might have to be untangled. Retrograde Jupiter would promise a sluggish cycle for business expansion, finances, and foreign travel. One way or another, retrograde motion offers a second chance, an opportunity to reconsider.

ARIES

*The year ahead for those
born under the sign of the Ram*
March 21–April 20

Your birth stars have blessed you with tremendous vitality and creative energy. Propelled forward and upward by this, you have the potential to scale great heights. Ancient astrologers illustrated these gifts with the image of the Ram, determined and aggressive, butting its head to defeat all obstacles. Born with the springtime, under the first sign of the zodiac, you approach life with a perpetual youthful zest.

With the vernal equinox Pluto changes direction in your 9th house of education, travel, and philosophy. New ideas, different surroundings, and associates from vastly different backgrounds broaden your perspective. You are apt to discard previously held concepts by All Fools' Day. You might visit a sacred site or have other spiritual experiences which have a consciousness transforming affect near your birthday. Late March through May Eve Mars will join Jupiter and Saturn in Taurus in your finance sector. Security issues need attention. Extra effort will be poured into sharpening salable job skills. There is a special item you long to purchase. Expect some tension regarding financial commitments. Try to enjoy all material blessings you do have, rather than regretting what may be lacking.

Air sign transits during mid-May through June promise interesting communication via E-mail, calls, and letters. A travel opportunity could be the topic. Respond quickly. These offers and opportunities can dissolve or be modified. *Carpe diem* should be your motto as Midsummer Day nears. When Jupiter enters Gemini on June 30 the full potential of this cosmic pattern will manifest.

Mars will aspect your Sun during July. Fortunately you adore excitement, because there will be plenty of it. Changing conditions at work, family members in flux planning different living arrangements indicate that the old ways are ending. New starts await you this summer, and you will be juggling a variety of projects. July brings three eclipses. These occur at the two New Moons on the 1st and 30th in Cancer and Leo and the Full Moon in Capricorn on the 16th. Be alert. Local and world news is rather electric. It is likely to be a pivotal time in many ways. With the important angular houses of your horoscope affected, you will be swept along in the drama. After August Eve your 3rd house is strong, with Saturn joining Jupiter there August 9. Through Yule this Saturn influence brings closer relationships with a brother, sister, classmates, or neighbors. Students should sharpen skills. A solid background which can be developed only by concentration and practice assures success in important studies or career challenges in the season to come.

September demands attention to detail and a stable routine. Others depend on you. Perform services with a cheerful heart and your rewards will come. Mercury opposes your natal Sun much of the month while your 6th house is highlighted by transits of the Sun and Mars. The ideas and needs of others can't be ignored. Focus on the very best health habits and diet. Make meals of fresh cider, autumn vegetables, and fruits as well as whole grains to cleanse and strengthen the body in the weeks before and after the autumn equinox.

October finds Uranus and Neptune turning direct completing retrograde cycles in Aquarius. The promise of the harmonious sextile they have been making to your Sun from the 11th house will finally manifest. Reach out to a new coven or meditation group. Spiritual or astrological studies can bring a new dimension to your life if pursued diligently. Take note of your dreams, make time for daily meditation from October through December. Messages from spirit guides and your higher self open new avenues of perception. For those who have been uncertain about goals, a purpose becomes clearer. The imagination is vivid. Neptune, planet of visions and fantasy, is affecting you potently. Direct this creativity constructively. Test ideas for substance and practicality before acting. October 15 Saturn retrogrades into Taurus where it will remain in your 2nd house through year's end. Recognize how true wealth is more than cash flow. Careful budgeting of resources is a must. Recycle and remodel. Almost magically, the dollars will stretch. Just after All Hallows' Eve your ruler, Mars, moves to oppose your Sun. Until late December this aspect makes others more assertive. Be low-key and diplomatic if dealing with difficult, volatile individuals. Wait and watch while visiting areas where there may be any hazards, tension, or environmental conditions to adapt to. Demand little, and offer guidance or suggestions with subtlety. Competitive individuals can take you by surprise. At Yule a Capricorn Sun-Mercury conjunction affects your 10th house. An eclipse December 25 highlights the specifics. Prepare for new developments at work. Experiment with a different approach in your profession. Your past performance means little. What you can offer currently is what will impress important people. You are the center of attention. Glow and shine during the dark, cold early days of winter. Your natural warmth and sparkle becomes a beacon of comfort to others. Simultaneously you light the way to new success on a personal level.

Venus crosses into your 12th house the first week of January where it will remain until February 2. Respect the tradition of secrecy in performing love rituals. It is best not to reveal the true depth and direction of your tender sentiments just now. January 9 brings an eclipse in your 4th house. Before the year's end you may seek a new residence. Family life is growing and changing. February 2 Venus enters Aries where it will remain through the end of winter. As the days lengthen, love blooms. Take time to express affection. Develop the artist within. Devote extra attention to cultural enrichment.

HEALTH

Acquaintances comment on your shining, expressive eyes. Aries has a special link to the head, face, and brain. Guard against eyestrain by taking bilberry herb as a supplement and soothing tired eyes with slices of cucumber. Near the time of the eclipses in July and again as winter begins you might have to cope with depression. Exercise followed by a soothing cup of St. John's wort tea should restore your usual upbeat energy level.

LOVE

Early in the year other projects and responsibilities can crowd love from your social calendar. On Friday, October 13th, a Full Moon in Aries marks an outpouring of love and admiration coming your way. You may be reunited with a soul mate from a past life near that date. The nurturing and joyful presence of Venus in your sign brings true happiness from Candlemas through the year's end.

FINANCE

Hold on to your money this year. Saturn is affecting your 2nd house. Be patient and purchase only what you can afford. Ignore a request for a loan or a high pressure sales pitch during the autumn. The urge to start a business or change careers strikes near the time of the New Moon in Aries on April 4 or with the eclipses following Midsummer Day and Yule. You can succeed if you persist. Add to your job knowledge and hone skills in preparation.

SPIRITUALITY

Companions are a source of example and inspiration now, for Neptune is in your 11th house. Arrange meetings with like-minded witches to honor the Moon's cycles and perform healing meditations.

TAURUS

*The year ahead for those
born under the sign of the Bull*
April 21–May 21

Reliability combined with power are hinted at by your emblem, the Bull. Hard work and determination are among your stellar qualities. As an earthy sign ruled by Venus, there is also a love of beauty and a subtle sensuality about you. You nurture all growing things and can become a spectacular gardener. Your love of beauty and comfort extends to a deep appreciation for music and the sounds of nature. Many Taureans keep songbirds or learn to sing and play instruments to revel in the sheer joy of pleasant sounds.

For the past couple of years Saturn, the ringed planet of reality and limitations, has been in your birth sign. You've had to conserve and make extra effort. Your state of mind has been very serious. This trend is finally drawing to a close. By August 9 Saturn crosses into Gemini and you will start to feel a sense of relief. During the final months of this long-term pattern, though, continue to follow the work ethic. Slowly but surely, you will notice progress and improvement in all areas of life.

Mars enters your birth sign just after the spring equinox. Exercise and fitness programs will appeal. It's easy to feel a bit tense and angry, but channel impatience into constructive outlets through May 3. On May Eve Mercury and Venus both enter your sign. Take special pains with your appearance. Social prospects and other opportunities abound through your birthday month. Make decisions about the fu-

ture, especially if travel or study are involved.

Your 2nd house is accented during June. You will devote energy and creativity to increasing income. There can be a new dimension to your work or more than one job. Financial planning absorbs your attention in the week before Midsummer Day. July's eclipses bring surprises from a family member. Your whole perception of how your family or extended family is structured may change. New philosophical concepts develop. An awareness of alternative thinking can emerge from conversations with those you respect. A journey might change your life. During August Jupiter and Saturn are both in your 2nd house. The need for financial security can become stronger. Devote Lammastide to prosperity rituals. On August 14–15 the Full Moon in Aquarius will activate Uranus in your 10th house. There can be some dreams or psychic experiences that relate to career. Be alert and respond quickly to the needs of the moment in your professional sphere. There could be a breakthrough allowing you greater freedom in the months to come. August ends with Venus moving into Libra, your 6th house, where it will remain through the autumn equinox. Health will be affected by your feelings toward friends and co-workers. Try color and sound therapies to alleviate mild ailments. They can work wonders.

October begins with Mercury making a long passage through Scorpio, your opposing sign. Through November 7 others will be very talkative. It's essential that you get both sides to every story. Take frequent breaks if it's hard to concentrate at work. The weeks before and after All Hallows' Eve will be quite hectic. Stay focused. The Full Moon on November 11 falls in Taurus. Take note of dreams and intuitions that night. They can guide you as this lunation ushers in a four-week cycle when you'll be the center of attention. A new talent emerges during the dull, dark days of late November. Saturn retrogrades into Taurus as autumn ends.

Yuletide finds you mulling over old decisions and completing outstanding obligations. Saturn turns direct the last week of January. A sense of somehow having paid your dues emerges. On January 26 Jupiter turns direct on the cusp of your 2nd house. It begins to trine several Aquarius planets in your 10th house. Finances are definitely on the upswing. Funds become available for a purchase you've wanted to make for a long time. A pay raise or return on an investment improves your lifestyle. A friend makes a recommendation or provides information which helps you realize a goal.

At Candlemas your 10th and 11th houses are both strong. Throughout February involvement with groups, selecting goals, and career aspirations will be important. Try doing meditations or affirmations with like-minded others. The sheer joy of the companionship coupled with the added strength of the group's energy will create a genuine magical force field which you can direct toward specific avenues of accomplishment by Valentine's Day. On February 15 Mars changes signs, moving into your 8th house where it will remain through the rest of the winter season. The detective in you comes out; you will spend time investigating and analyzing. Curiosity about the afterlife sharpens. You might visit the scene of a past life or connect with a soul mate whom you've known before. Seances can be successful beyond your wildest expectations, for the spirit world is especially active and responsive now. On March 9 your ruler, Venus, turns retrograde. Get plenty of rest through the spring equinox. Vitality can be a bit low. Habit is always a strong guiding force in your life. Be aware of counterproductive habits and resolve to break them. Be gentle and tolerant with loved ones. Casual friendships are under better stars than is a grand passion.

HEALTH

Develop good habits and stick to them. It isn't always easy for you to exercise and eat a light diet, for you are sensual. You revel in creature comforts and delectable flavors. Be aware of how others affect your health and well-being from late December – mid-February when Mars is oppose your Sun. Saturn is leaving your birth sign this year. Chronic health conditions are about to clear up. Efforts made to take care of health now will definitely be rewarded next year.

LOVE

Beltane marks a happy love cycle, for Venus enters your sign for several weeks then. The Full Moon in November is another celestial influence which will make Cupid smile, for it will shed light upon your charisma and beauty from November 11– December 10. A retrograde Venus from March 9 through the spring equinox can rekindle an old flame. Proceed with caution, for what happened before will happen again. Your 12th house is involved, so quiet acts of charity and kindness can be most rewarding. Be subtle and patient regarding open declarations of love at winter's end.

FINANCE

Jupiter and Saturn flirt with the cusp of your money sector all year. Hard work will be a must, but there is potential for financial improvement. You always treasure lovely possessions and insist upon the best quality. Don't be tempted to overextend. Purchase only what you can pay for or there could be a problem with credit cards and debt after Yule. Explore new sources of income and sharpen salable job skills. You are in demand. It's better to depend upon your own earnings rather than the income from a partner or investments this year.

SPIRITUALITY

Neptune's transit through your 10th house makes you long to bring a spiritual atmosphere to your job. Give your workplace a Feng Shui treatment. Add a small fountain to your desk or hang an octagon-shaped mirror on the wall opposite your office door.

GEMINI

*The year ahead for those
born under the sign of the Twins*
May 22–June 21

The symbolism of all that is dual describes you. Others find you intriguing because there's always a new facet of your nature to discover. You are imaginative with a delicious sense of humor and a lively brilliance. The emblem of the Twins hints at your skill in the art of communication. All activities involving the spoken or written word are your forte.

Mercury is dashing through your 10th house from the spring equinox until April 12. Your career is changing shape and focus. There might be new job duties or travel involved. Publications, workshops, and seminars linked to your profession can keep you on top of the new demands. April 13 until May Eve first the Aries Sun, then Mercury and Venus sextile you from your 11th house. Friends return favors and put in a kind word; you will be preoccupied with thoughts of the future. New goals and desires are crystallizing. The first week of May Mars enters your sign where it will remain until June 16. This is a dynamic cycle of motivation. Higher energy and enthusiasm lead you toward great accomplishments, yet you must exercise discretion. A quick display of anger or recklessness can sacrifice all the fruits of your labors in an instant. Self-control is a must. Venus will brighten your life near your birthday. Expect a happy start to your new year. Take time to nurture a friendship and beautify your surroundings.

With Midsummer Day an alignment of planets in your 2nd house turns your thoughts toward finances, comfort, and security. In the wee hours on June 30 Jupiter enters your sign for a year-long stay. This largest of planets always points to wider horizons and growth. You may accept more work or develop a new salable skill with thoughts of boosting your income. There can be much more travel coming up. Mercury turns retrograde the last week of June through July 18. Energy fluctuates; don't worry if you need extra rest. Projects can take longer than planned, so be patient. Avoid unfamiliar territory of all kinds while Mercury is retrograde. The eclipse of July 30 combined with several Leo transits accents your 3rd house. Be diplomatic and discreet in all communication. There might be a transportation situation to resolve at Lammastide. A sibling or neighbor needs emotional support or other considerations.

In early August Saturn touches the cusp of your sign where it will remain until October 15. This heralds a serious mood. It's time to take stock of how you are using valuable resources. Remedy any serious problems in the foundation of your life to avoid consequences next year. A new awareness of the passage of time subtly affects you. The last three weeks of August Venus affects your home and family sector. Add art pieces and new furnishings to your house; conduct real estate transactions. Plan a pre-Labor Day party and invite all of your favorite people. It's a great time to entertain. During September both Jupiter and Saturn turn retrograde in your birth sign. Some loose ends from the past demand attention before you can move forward. Be aware of the force of tradition and habit as the autumnal equinox passes. On October 19 Mercury goes retrograde and Venus joins Pluto in Sagittarius to oppose your Sun.

Through All Hallows' Eve relationships are changing. Listen and observe in order to understand others. A question of legality or propriety might have to be addressed. Follow good health habits. Early November through Yuletide Mars will transit Libra, adding warmth to your love and pleasure sector. A memorable vacation can bring much happiness; a new hobby or love affair adds joy. You find a way to realize a cherished wish. The Full Moon in your own sign of Gemini on December 11 brings the specifics into focus. That night is also a good one for rituals involving personal growth or health needs.

The solar eclipse on December 25 can bring some changes in financial planning. Review tax matters, insurance coverage, and investments as the year ends. Astral journeys can open a new awareness of the afterlife in your sleep as December ends. The first week of January finds Venus gliding into your 10th house where it will remain through Candlemas. You will enjoy the companionship of professional associates. Social events impact your career. Allow your natural charm and beauty to shine at work. Presentations you give before groups now can open new doorways. The retrograde Mercury in Pisces February 4–26 brings in a hectic cycle. Double-check instructions and agreements. There can be some confusing situations involving a job. Control stress and don't cram too many activities into limited time frames. From the end of February through March (until the eve of the spring equinox), Mercury, Uranus, and Neptune are all beautifully aspected. They will trine your Sun from your 9th house. Imported foods or artwork and clothing from other lands can brighten winter's end. Contact with those from another land would enrich your life. It's a perfect time to study a foreign language or enroll in an educational program. Travel during March would open new vistas which could literally alter the course of your life. Consider visiting a sacred site.

HEALTH
The Full Moon in Scorpio, the sign which rules your health sector, on May 18 brings insights into the current state of your health. Be sensitive to messages sent by your body. Since a water sign relates to your health, be sure to drink plenty of fresh spring water. Relaxing by the sea or at the lakefront can do wonders for your well-being. This year transit Pluto will oppose your Sun, the source of life and vitality. This shows that surroundings and companions will impact your health. Avoid people and places which make you feel ill for any reason.

LOVE
Venus transits near your birthday and again in September bring romantic promise. Mars, planet of desire, will be in your love sector from November 4 until December 23. That time period should add some sparkle to your social life. You long for companions who are interesting and stimulating. Try using fragrance to heighten your charisma this year. Lavender, musk, or patchouli are aromas that could create a loving atmosphere. Place your favorite oil on your pulse points, then use it to dress a rose candle which you will burn while concentrating on matters of the heart.

FINANCE
The Moon rules your 2nd house of finances. Be aware of how the lunar phases impact income and spending power. The Moon relates to changes and emotions, so there is a changeable quality to your budget. Finances are a highly emotional topic. The triple eclipse at the New and Full Moons in July will be most significant. Focus on money matters then. Jupiter's passage into your own sign this year should bring growth and opportunity, but it's followed closely by Saturn. This could drive up expenses as well as income. Patience and steadiness will help.

SPIRITUALITY
Inspirational words will be instrumental in stimulating spiritual awareness. Collect favorite poems, mantras, and chants. Reciting these with a coven of sympathetic companions will elevate your consciousness. You can be inspired by metaphysical and craft books. Peruse ancient texts as well as modern publications about the craft and other spiritual traditions.

CANCER

The year ahead for those
born under the sign of the Crab
June 22–July 23

Ruled by the Moon, you have a sensitive and sentimental nature. The moods of the people and places which surround you are mirrored by your expressive, responsive facial features. The sea always bewitches you. Your emblem, the Crab, reveals your special affinity for the magic of water. As the Crab carries its home on its back, you are attached to your home, often extending it to include your work and other areas of life.

The vernal equinox finds Mercury passing through your sister water sign of Pisces while making a favorable trine to your Sun. This pattern stimulates the tongue as well as the brain, and continues through the first half of April. You'll feel drawn toward imported items, other lands, different religious and philosophical concepts. Those who wish to write or who are speakers or teachers will enjoy an especially productive time as spring begins. During April Mars enters Taurus and will conjoin Jupiter and Saturn, affecting your 11th house. Competition arises within your social circle. Friends and enemies are hard to define and might change roles. Flexibility helps release any anger or uncertainty about the future. Near May Eve the alignment of Taurus planets strengthens with Venus, the Sun, and Mercury joining Mars, Jupiter, and Saturn in that sign. A great sensitivity to the Earth develops. Rituals calling upon nature goddesses, Pan, or the Green Man are apropos. Ecology and animals can be-come a part of your life this spring. You can be profoundly impacted by involvement in group and community activities.

June accents your 12th house with Venus, the Sun, and Mars transits. The inner planes and the secret depths of the psyche are active. You will become more introspective and will cherish privacy. A need to avoid confrontation and a new appreciation for peace and quiet develops. There are some temporary blockages in expressing love openly. One you admire might be preoccupied or otherwise unable to return affection. Those near you may experience some health challenges. Be patient. Direct pent-up emotions constructively through arts and crafts or music. Jupiter will enter Gemini June 30 where it will remain through the remainder of the year. This assures support and help from hidden or unexpected avenues, probably when most needed. Seek solitude to heal the mind and body. A new connection to wilderness areas and untamed animals can deepen spiritual growth. There will be several opportunities by Yule to quietly extend kindness. If these seem to go unacknowledged, rest assured that the seeds sown will bring eventual karmic rewards.

July has three eclipses. Expect some major upsets in the status quo. A new home or job can be in the works. Don't deny the wisdom of changing and growing. Be sensitive to messages from your body for the rest of the year. Health and fitness programs can enhance longevity and quality of life. Volatile Mars will transit your sign during this eclipse cycle. Direct energy wisely. Avoid controversy and confrontations. Tread with caution; don't light any fires in haste.

Saturn hovers on the cusp of your 12th house when it touches the zero degree of Gemini just after Lammastide. This lasts until mid-October when it retrogrades into Taurus. This trend points to the needs of those much older or younger. Be kind and charitable. Affirm the positive. If feelings of loneliness or melancholy get out of control, you can suffer unnecessarily. It is possible to create either your own happiness or misery under this Saturn influence.

Mercury will transit through Scorpio from September 28, after the autumnal equinox, until December 3. Since it trines your Sun from the 5th house, children progress, communicate well, and will be a source of joy. This favorable aspect is strongest near All Hallows' Eve when it is supported by the Scorpio Sun. Romantic liaisons generate travel or learning opportunities. Create with language–you're imaginative in applying the spoken or written word.

Autumn concludes with a potent dose of Mars energies. The red planet will transit Libra in your 4th house from early November through the winter solstice. You'll feel motivated to improve your residence. Family dynamics can be in an uproar. Loved ones seem complex and demanding. Look for solutions rather than giving way to anger. On December 23 Mars moves into Scorpio. Suddenly, solutions to dilemmas develop. Through mid-February it will make a delightful trine aspect in your 5th house. Expect to enjoy more athletic and competitive leisure time pursuits. Love will have added zest. An admirer becomes more attentive. This peaks with the eclipse in Cancer at the Full Moon on January 9. The two weeks following the eclipse will usher in changes which set the pace for the months to come. After Candlemas, February 2, Mercury retrogrades into Aquarius, your 8th house, where it will remain through mid-March. Others discuss finances. Your curiosity is piqued about the afterlife and past life experiences. It's a marvelous time to try regressive hypnosis or astral projection. On March 9 Venus turns retrograde and creates some havoc in the 10th house through the end of winter. Use humor to soothe difficult or ill-mannered co-workers. Postpone asking for a raise or changing jobs. Take pride in doing daily tasks as well as possible and be patient. Recognition will come later.

HEALTH

With Saturn stirring up your 11th house all year, be aware of how other people affect your health. Protect against contagious colds or infections by washing your hands often. Keep a physical distance from those who seem ill. Get inoculations as needed. The eclipse pattern underscores vitality during July and January. Pluto is in your 6th house. Daily routine and the work environment impact your health. Make certain your employment conditions are wholesome. You can release stress through regular exercise.

LOVE

Sharing meals and enjoying home and hearth can provide the perfect backdrop for romance. Use a beloved family heirloom such as a handmade quilt or antique vase, or perhaps prepare a recipe handed down from grandma to generate an ambience of love. Venus transits your sign Midsummer Eve–July 13. This promises a cycle of romantic happiness and popularity. Relationships move to a new level at the Full Moon eclipse in January.

FINANCE

Your professional dedication and loyalty make you a treasure to work with. A conscientious sensitivity toward others gives you a flair for public relations and other people-oriented work. Throughout most of the year ahead, Jupiter in Taurus will sextile your Sun. This shows offers and opportunities coming from helpful people. Define financial goals. How far you actually progress depends upon following through. The eclipse on July 30 affects your 2nd house. This promises changes in sources of income. An industry could change. Stay in touch with shifting trends. Update your job knowledge and skills to assure success.

SPIRITUALITY

Create an altar or meditation corner in your own home. This will assist you in connecting with the Lord and Lady and incorporating them into all facets of your life. A small sanctuary in the garden, especially if a pool or fountain is nearby, can do wonders to help you feel the presence of the Old Ones.

LEO

The year ahead for those
born under the sign of the Lion
July 24–August 23

There is a regal quality about you. Wherever you go you are noticed. Generosity and a warm kindness characterize you. You are excellent as an executive and in working with young people. Your enthusiasm and cheerfulness allow you to be a wonderful role model. Ruled by the Sun, you have an affinity for light and sunshine. Those near you will bask in the brightness you create.

Throughout the entire spring Jupiter and Saturn in Taurus will be affecting your 10th house, accenting career aspirations. You will be concerned about professional productivity and advancement. Dedicated hard work combined with patience will be the best route to the rewards you seek. At the vernal equinox Mercury and Venus are in your 8th house. This shows an interest in analysis and research work. A puzzle is solved by All Fools' Day. Through April 12 communication with the inner planes and spirit world will be clear. Trust premonitions and heed dreams. The remainder of April finds Aries transits impacting your 9th house while trine your Sun. You will enjoy wandering distant frontiers of the mind as well as planning actual journeys. Students will reach a new level of understanding. Meditation sessions mark advances into a higher level of consciousness. A gathering of planets at your midheaven in May spotlights your work. The glimmer of natural star quality brings added praise and appreciation in the weeks following Beltane.

The first half of June Mars will sextile your Sun from the 11th house. Friends will be a source of encouragement. Social prospects are promising. Through the remainder of June several planets including Mercury will accent the 12th house. You will seek more peace and privacy. The inner life becomes more active. When Mercury goes retrograde just after Midsummer Day this uncharacteristic reserve will deepen. On July 13 Venus enters your own sign. Through Lammastide social prospects are wonderful. You will be cherished and charming. Creative projects involving the use of color will progress well. Late July promises change and excitement. Be flexible and progressive for there is an eclipse in your sign on July 30.

Travel prospects are marvelous during August as Mercury and Mars will move rapidly through Leo. Your mind is agile and alert, much will be accomplished near your birthday. As the autumn equinox approaches, Virgo and Libra transits affect your 2nd and 3rd houses. New ideas about financial planning will attract. A neighbor offers helpful advice. Jupiter turns retrograde on September 29. By All Hallows' Eve this brings a different circle of friends and new priorities into focus. October 19–November 12 Venus will move through your love sector. Romantic involvements have a new tenderness and zest. An attractive person will shows signs of wanting to move closer. Scorpio transits during October and November can make you feel discontented with your home. With the bright and cool days of autumn you might long for new furnishings or even seek a new residence entirely. Wait until after November 8 to sign leases or real estate contracts, though. Mercury completes its retrograde on that date and the rest of the month is better for making a major change. Sudden decisions made from mid-to-late October can leave uncertainty or regrets in their wake. Reconsider and look at all the options. The last three weeks of November finds Venus in your 6th house. Love for animal friends deepens. A new cat or bird could adopt you. Health will improve if you follow a low stress yet productive schedule and focus on employment you truly enjoy.

During December Venus will join Uranus in Aquarius, your opposing sign. In the days leading up to the Yuletide holiday others will be unpredictable; intimate relationships will be changing. Allow companions to express their needs and give them plenty of freedom. Recognize that all types of relationships must grow and change to remain truly alive. If someone does leave, accept that this will leave a space for someone new to come in. The eclipses on December 25 and January 9 affect your 6th and 12th houses. Health can be important as the winter grows cold and long. Take care of physical needs. Revel in creature comforts such as warm meals and thick sweaters. Loved ones might seek your guidance and support in the face of a health or employment challenge. Offer all the strength and assistance possible.

When the Sun enters Aquarius on January 20 companions will take more initiative and show greater confidence. At Candlemas Mercury completes a square with Saturn in other fixed signs. Your workload will lighten and it's easier to be optimistic. With the Leo Full Moon on February 8 you will begin a four-week cycle of great sensitivity. Psychic insights will be rich and meaningful. Take time to listen to the small, still voice within. Perform a ritual designed to amplify personal strength and success. The retrograde Mercury of February 4–26 in Aquarius shows uncertainty surfacing in others. Allow them to change plans and opinions. Mars will transit your 5th house of love and leisure from February 15 through the vernal equinox. Active hobbies will appeal. There can be a competitive mood surrounding romance as well as recreation. Don't let an incident of teasing or the involvement in sports and games go too far. Keep a sense of balance and perspective and the winter will end on a positive note.

HEALTH
The eclipse pattern this year profoundly impacts your health. This is especially true of the Capricorn eclipses on July 16 and December 25. Be aware of changes within your body. Comfortable clothing apropos to climate and temperature can be most helpful. Relax with a cup of hot catnip tea when stress builds. Don't neglect health care. Follow good habits involving diet and exercise.

LOVE
Unpredictable Uranus transits your 7th house of relationships all year. New liaisons can form and old ones dissolve. If you prefer to grow with the same partner allow your beloved to explore and express a bit of independence. Venus transits your sign July 14–August 6. Celestial patterns smile on your love life then. The New Moon on January 24 marks the start of another important four-week cycle regarding partnerships and commitment. Lammas and Candlemas are both ideal sabbats to devote to love magic.

FINANCE
Scrimping and saving is alien to you. Being surrounded with quality and opulence comes naturally. Often Lions go through a phase of accumulating debts and juggling bills until they learn the wisdom of reasonable budgeting. The last year has found both Jupiter and Saturn square your Sun, indicating some financial hurdles. On July 1 Jupiter enters Gemini and will sextile you. Saturn follows a few weeks later. By autumn you will be in much better financial circumstances than you have enjoyed in many moons. Pursue opportunities and learn from a past faux pas.

SPIRITUALITY
Neptune is in opposition to your Sun the year long. This promises contact with an influential spiritual leader or role model. Group meditation or ritual sessions can uplift you. At the same time, Neptune can represent confusion as well as inspiration. Strive to see those whom you admire clearly. Balance advice you are offered with the dictates of your own heart and mind. The study of spiritual poetry, sacred texts, and ancient music provides insight.

VIRGO

*The year ahead for those
born under the sign of the Virgin*
August 24–September 23

The archetype of the spinster is descriptive of Virgos of both sexes. Originally the word "spinster" meant literally one who could spin. It indicated a special and talented person. Spinsters won admiration and respect. Virgo people desire to be of service, to be devoted to a worthy cause. Quiet and modest, you don't usually give yourself fully to anyone. This self-sufficiency becomes both a magnet and a barrier in social situations. You have many admirers, yet can keep them at a distance. An orderly home or work environment is essential for you to reach your highest potential. Noise and disorder can devastate you.

From the vernal equinox through Midsummer Day Jupiter will be in Taurus, your sister earth sign, trine to your Sun. Profit-making potential and growth on every level are indicated. Springtime is ideal for travel, as your 9th house is involved. March 20 through early April Mercury and Venus will oppose you. Listen to suggestions; compromise if a debate ensues. An admirer seeks your company. Mars is favorable from late March through May Eve. You will be more energetic and motivated. A competitive mood drives you. The first half of May an alignment of planets in Taurus in your 9th house can find you planning extensive travel, eyeing educational programs, or trying your hand at writing. If you have a book in your mind and heart, it might manifest now. The first three weeks of June can be hectic, for Gemini planets cross your midheaven and square your Sun. Others expect much of you; you're at the center of activity. Try creative ideas and group discussion at work. Focus on efficient use of time and resources.

By the summer solstice you will receive some compliments. Mercury, your ruler, is retrograde June 24–July 18 in Cancer, affecting your 11th house. Old friends may call. An interest which captivated you long ago suddenly intrigues again. The eclipse of July 16 affects your 5th house of love. A change of heart is due. New ideas about love and romance are in the wind. Explore, but postpone making a binding decision regarding commitment until after Lammastide. During August, Pluto completes its retrograde in your 4th house. Memories of childhood experiences can be processed and understood. Needs concerning housing surface. Adjustments are about to be made regarding living arrangements. From August 7–30 Venus brightens your sign. Love prospects hold great promise. Develop ways to beautify yourself as well as your surroundings. The first week of September a Mercury influence favors discussion and decision making. Throughout the remainder of the month transits accent the 2nd house. The urge to expand earning capacity is growing. The reality of financial needs will motivate you to seek additional income. Request a raise or sharpen skills to make yourself more valuable as an employee.

Mars enters Virgo just before the autumn equinox and will remain there until November 3. This promises an exciting six weeks. Enthusiasm and courage build; you attempt ambitious projects and pursue a dream. There can be some anger and impatience to quell, though. If annoyed, seek ways to resolve the situation. Past life studies and traditional celebrations can characterize Halloween this year, for Mercury will be retrograde mid-October until early November. The colorful, crisp autumn days will be marked by a certain nostalgia and a sensitivity to the patterns which shape your life. After November 8 the mood shifts. Through the end of November Scorpio and

Capricorn transits will trine and sextile your Sun, bringing in positive 3rd and 5th house influences. A new hobby or love affair brings pleasure. Attend a concert, art show, or theatrical production. Short journeys are exhilarating and successful.

The weeks before Yuletide find a strong mutable sign influence affecting you, with squares from both Gemini and Sagittarius transits. You will strive to balance professional and domestic responsibilities. Get organized and focus on managing time and priorities. You could find working at home a worthwhile solution. The eclipses at the end of December and beginning of January affect your love and friendship houses. New faces enter your circle; old ones may move on. There will be a spirit of restlessness as winter deepens. You will want more from life but will have to strive to identify exactly what that means.

Health will be important during the last half of January, for your ruling planet, Mercury, will join Neptune and Uranus in your 6th house. You will enjoy learning more about health. Healing could occur through the use of Reiki or other alternative techniques. Protect yourself from inclement weather. After Candlemas Mercury turns retrograde, bringing a recurrence of health-related interests. A karmic bond with an animal companion becomes important during February. Extra rest is the best gift you can give yourself. The Full Moon in your own birth sign of Virgo on March 9 is coupled with the start of a retrograde Venus. The last weeks of winter heighten emotions and sensitivity. Learn from the past. Be patient in matters of the heart. Study Tarot, interpret dreams, read tea leaves, and observe omens during March.

HEALTH

Your birth sign has always had a special association with health. It's your favorite topic and often a perfect career choice. All year Uranus and Neptune in Aquarius will transit your 6th house. Experimental methods of healing are worth pursuing. Be aware of the role faith has in wellness. Good or bad, an illness may not be as it first seems. There is a mysterious situation developing regarding health. Get a second opinion if in doubt about a diagnosis. The winter months bring important turning points in health conditions. The health of companions can affect you. Spend time with those who are robust.

LOVE

The eclipses this year dramatically affect your love sector. Expect changes in loyalties and preferences. You will discover new ways to express tender feelings. You will be inclined to want more zest and adventure in your love life. August and November can be especially happy with regard to romantic interludes. Pluto's influence shows that a family member might affect your social life. A family event could provide the backdrop for getting to know a new love.

FINANCE

While Saturn and Jupiter transit Taurus from early spring through June, your attitude concerning finance will be sound. These two friendly earth sign giants will aid your judgement and values. Plan for the future and make investments then. Mutable sign influences grow stronger as the year passes. You might be tempted to diversify or gamble with security in some way from autumn through the winter months. Keep a nest egg to rely on. Expect to choose between a secure income or more glamour and glitz at work.

SPIRITUALITY

As your emblem, the Virgin, hints, purity and idealism are important in your belief system. The proper form and attention to detail will help you to find meaning in spiritual ceremonies. Harvest festivals are especially beautiful and meaningful for you. Honor the Lord and Lady with altar decorations of autumn foliage. Share fall fruits, vegetables, and whole grain breads at Lammas, the autumn equinox, and All Hallows' feasts.

LIBRA

*The year ahead for those
born under the sign of the Scales*
September 24–October 23

With Venus as your ruler, you are known for your courtesy and charm. It seems effortless for you to look beautiful. This is an illusion, however. You actually put much thought and care into creating the ideal image. Marriage and other partnerships are always a focus. It isn't natural for you to spend much time alone. The celestial Scales illustrate your affinity for justice and your quest for balance. As the Scales are the only inanimate emblem in the zodiac, this hints at a special refinement. Many in the legal and military fields have Libra planets prominent in their horoscopes. You instinctively appreciate the value of reconciliation and mediation as a way to resolve almost all difficulties.

Throughout the year expect sparkle and good times regarding romance. Uranus and Neptune will transit your 5th house and trine your Sun. This pattern also helps creative ability develop. A new avocation will enrich your life this year. As the vernal equinox passes Mars enters Taurus, your 8th house. As springtime progresses Mars is joined there by Mercury, Venus, Jupiter, Saturn, and the Sun. This potent collection of energy will draw karmic experiences. There is a new awareness of how fate operates. Past life studies will be truly profound during April and May. At the same time, managing inherited or invested money can affect financial planning. Others impact your security. Be leery of financial advice if it clashes with your own good

sense. The Full Moon in Libra early on April 18 brings the specifics into focus. That lunation is a wonderful time to seek closure on issues of which you are growing weary.

May 15 through June transits in Gemini and Aquarius create a grand trine in air with your Sun. Life will lighten up. A new perspective dissolves old heartaches or disappointments by Midsummer Day. July's triple eclipses will bring some changes in the way you balance career with home life. A new dream emerges while an old desire is abandoned. Be alert to new trends affecting your profession in July. Don't become outdated. A conversation with someone younger or less experienced can refresh your career performance. August finds Saturn joining Jupiter in Gemini. Both planets trine you from the 9th house. Widen your horizons with travel and the study of other belief systems. This aspect strengthens you on every level. Health improves after Lammas.

September begins with Mercury transiting rapidly through your sign. New ideas help solve problems. You will speak and write eloquently while thinking quickly. Stress melts away. Mars enters Virgo and crosses the cusp of your 12th house September 17. Open confrontations make you shudder. You will be especially subtle during the weeks ahead. You will cherish thoughts and feelings within, yet express little. A psychic connection with an animal or a meaningful dream may provide a pivotal experience near your birthday. Neptune completes its retrograde in October highlighting your love and pleasure sector. Confused passions clear up. You're intuitive and creative, yet can brush away illusion's cobwebs. Imaginative use of music, color, and art allows you to add beauty to your world as All Hallows' Eve nears.

November begins with several planets retrograde in the money houses. Look at established financial patterns critically. Pay off old debts before shopping for new purchases during the week following Halloween. A Taurus Full Moon on November 11 shines on how shared finances affect your money matters. Mars enters Libra in November. You'll feel more assertive and enthusiastic. There's a highly motivated and progressive cycle urging you on. The last half of November a Venus square generates sentiment and sensitivity. You expect much from others. Delectable sweet treats are irresistible. If you indulge, exercise away the added pounds or the eclipse on December 25 can find you voicing regrets. The last week of December Mercury and the Sun in Capricorn affect your 4th house. This generates a new phase involving residence and relatives. You might plan to redecorate or remodel. The purchase of a second home or a move is very possible.

January brings plenty of 5th house activity with first Venus, then Mercury and the Sun joining Uranus and Neptune in Aquarius. Children will be a source of delight. Shared ideas and interests with a loved one deepen a special relationship. Jupiter is direct after January 26 in Gemini. Travel plans materialize near Candlemas, for this affects the 9th house. Spiritual insights received through study and discussion groups offer valuable guidance. Read a new book suggested by a friend. The retrograde Mercury in February brings an opportunity to reconnect with a lost love or understand past relationships. Complete neglected creative projects. After Valentine's Day Mars enters your 3rd house. Expect more commuter travel and interesting communications. On March 9 Venus turns retrograde in Aries, your opposing sign. Be very tolerant of others through the spring equinox. Humor is essential. It can neutralize potentially awkward or hurtful situations. Draw upon the wisdom of past experiences during the last days of winter. Be aware of your natural inclinations and gifts. The path of least resistance leads to success in March.

HEALTH
Neptune rules your health sector. Health matters can be surrounded with elements of mystery and controversy. Always stay well-informed about medical conditions and seek a second opinion. Dreams and intuition can guide you toward good health. This year Neptune's position points toward leisure time activities impacting health. During vacations, engage in fitness programs. Look into a stay at a spa or meditation retreat.

LOVE
Equality is an important part of a healthy relationship for you. Fairness is something you both seek and offer. The respect for balance extends to lifestyle, and you are happiest when able to divide your time equally between love and other obligations. August 31–September 24 Venus will move through your birth sign. Existing relationships deepen and improve. If alone, circulate and reach out just before the autumn equinox. There will be a special someone who cares.

FINANCE
In recent years you have overextended a bit financially. A loved one probably needed some financial assistance, too. On June 30 Jupiter enters Gemini ushering in the best prosperity cycle you've known in many moons. Since the 9th house is affected, experiment with prosperity affirmations, spells, and rituals. There's a new awareness of how attitude affects income and opportunities. Educational programs aimed at boosting earning power can be very worthwhile. Your natural artistic ability is also enhanced by this trend. Develop a creative idea, for it can bring unexpected hidden gains by Yuletide.

SPIRITUALITY
Travel always opens new vistas of spiritual awareness for you. Visit temples, mystical sites, and sacred ground in other lands. Discuss philosophical concepts with those who follow a different faith or craft tradition. Collect ghost stories and learn about the archaeology of early peoples. This will deepen your own sensitivity to other dimensions.

SCORPIO

*The year ahead for those
born under the sign of the Scorpion*
October 24–November 22

Passion blended with energy are the keynotes of your nature. Ruled by mysterious and remote Pluto, there is an intensity and subtlety to all of your actions. Superficiality in any form will win your disapproval. Directing and controlling your emotional drives toward positive ends is an important task which must not be neglected if you are to reach your brightest potential. You are comfortable with the concept of death. Past life study as well as contact with other dimensions and the afterlife will add depth and meaning to your existence. Dedicating your life to a worthwhile cause would give you great satisfaction.

The early days of spring, from the vernal equinox through April 6, find Venus and Mercury dancing through your love sector. You will enjoy talking and thinking about romance. Sharing vacation plans or creative projects can help deepen existing relationships. If unattached near All Fools' Day a special someone can become a part of your life. Throughout the rest of April until the week following Beltane, Mars moves through Taurus along with Saturn and Jupiter, in opposition to your Sun. Expect some competition. Others will be assertive. Request few favors; be accepting. Avoid legal entanglements if at all possible. A troubled person might need your comfort and counsel. The Full Moon falls in Scorpio May 18. This brings intentions into the open. It's a favorable time for dream work and meditation as psychic energies are high and the gateway to the other side stands open. The last ten days of May four Gemini transits activate your 8th house. Financial matters, including investments, can be studied and discussed. An old mystery is cleared up.

During June Mercury will glide through your 9th house at a trine to your Sun. There can be some interesting travel opportunities. It's a good time to review language skills. Writers enjoy a productive time. On June 16 Mars enters Cancer. This planet co-rules your birth sign and has tremendous impact on you. By the summer solstice you will notice its sparkle. Expect to have more energy, enthusiasm, motivation, and ideas. This stays in force through the end of July. On June 30 Jupiter enters Gemini where it will remain through the rest of the year. This promises financial expansion and opportunity. A tax refund, investment return, inheritance, or other windfall should improve money matters in the months to come. July's triple eclipse pattern will affect your 3rd, 4th, and 9th houses. New philosophical concepts may change previously held beliefs. Conversations and letters are apt to be unusual and interesting. You could consider a real estate transaction or move to a new apartment. At Lammastide Mars joins the Sun and Venus in Leo. Early August emphasizes heritage and family life. Meetings with relatives, redecorating, or entertaining at home can be a focus. On August 21 Pluto, your ruler, finishes a long retrograde. By the month's end a new sense of purpose and focus will develop. You will feel especially connected to the mass karma and consciousness of those who are a part of your community.

September finds Venus hiding in your 12th house. This trend is in force until just past the autumn equinox. An unrequited love might have to be resolved. Hidden desires and attractions live in the dark, deep reservoirs of your heart. Don't assume others know how you feel. It might be necessary to express emotions more openly. You can do great kindnesses to those who are truly in need this month. Goodness assures an unexpected reward for you in the end. October begins with Mercury in your sign. You will be alert and observant, absorbing and using new information. Until October 19 travel is favored. Mercury is retrograde after that. Late October through November 8 favors completing old tasks and reviewing forgotten information. Any type of refresher course you need would be worthwhile near All Hallows' Eve.

November finds Mars entering your 12th house. You will avoid confrontation. Your natural aura of mystery deepens as your birthday month unfolds. As the late autumn days shorten you will be more adept than ever at conducting investigations and moving in secret. On November 12 Venus enters your 3rd house and will sextile your Sun through December 8. You will present ideas to others in an irresistible way. Your writing and speaking ability can carry you far. A sibling or neighbor draws closer and expresses genuine admiration and affection.

Just after Yule Mars enters your own sign of Scorpio. You will be more expressive and fiery. Much can be accomplished if you exercise control and keep perspective. You will be active and dynamic. This potent transit lasts through Valentine's Day. At the same time the eclipses of December and January affect transportation and education. The winter can find you pursuing new studies or planning an important journey. After Candlemas Venus will enter your health sector. You will be aware of the role love and comfort play in physical health. Music, fragrance, and color can be incorporated into a fitness regime. Don't underestimate the therapeutic value of new finery or a new coiffure. Put effort into looking well and delighting the senses. Healing will occur as winter ends.

HEALTH

Mars and Aries rule health in your birth chart. You can benefit from trying new and experimental treatments. There is a tendency toward aggressive therapies, though. Always remember the role that time and patience play in the healing process. Be kind to yourself when not feeling quite well. The Full Moon on Friday, October 13 affects your 6th house of health. During the four weeks following that lunation you can gain a deeper understanding of health needs, discovering what is essential to maintaining good health.

LOVE

Forgiveness and overcoming jealousy are hurdles Scorpions must face at some point in their lives. Once you transmute these baser feelings into a higher form of love, the way will be cleared for you to achieve your most important goal in life, that of connecting deeply and intimately with the right person. Venus transits indicate that September 25–October 19 and January 4–February 2 are your most promising love cycles this year. A love ritual performed at Candlemas should be especially effective. Call upon the Lady in her guise as Freya. Incorporate cat symbolism into magical workings, in honor of the gray cats which draw Freya's chariot.

FINANCE

Jupiter, ruler of your 2nd house, will enter your 8th house when it changes signs at the end of June. Both of these sectors link to finances. This transit should usher in a year of better financial prospects. Saturn will also touch the cusp of your 8th house briefly August 10–October 15. That time span brings you insight about upcoming financial situations. Careful analysis and preparation then will assure your financial success over the next few years.

SPIRITUALITY

Feeling comfortable with and understanding the afterlife and the processes of life and death will always be at the core of your spiritual needs. If you have an opportunity to witness either a birth or a death you can experience a profound spiritual awakening. Neptune's position this year encourages you to bring spiritual energies into your home. Try candle burning and incense to welcome their presence.

SAGITTARIUS

The year ahead for those
born under the sign of the Archer
November 23–December 21

Just as the Archer aims at ever distant targets, Sagittarians seek to forever enlarge the parameters of their lives. Your happy-go-lucky attitude and fertile mind give you a distinctive charm. You love to offer advice to others. The clergy, teaching, law, and medicine are all professions which can be rewarding for this reason. You're apt to tempt fate with an occasional risk or gamble. Exploring new horizons of the mind as well as the physical environment make you an incurable optimist. Animals are especially important to you. Your sign has a half-human and half-animal motif to hint at this heartfelt bond. You have an affinity for large canines and horses.

Pluto will transit the middle degrees of your birth sign all year long. A deep transformation is in progress. New potentials are being unearthed; projects begun this year could alter the course of your life. The vernal equinox finds Venus and Mercury in your home and real estate sector. Through All Fools' Day you will be thinking about your residence or feel that you're living in two places at once. Jupiter, your ruling planet, is in Taurus from the beginning of the year through June 30. This is wonderful for physical fitness and healing. Concentrate on overcoming any ills of the psyche or body through the springtime. April 6–30 Venus is in your 5th house of love and romance. In your brother fire sign of Aries, this transit holds the promise of new joy. Work on existing relationships or reach out to someone new who has caught your fancy.

Expect a warm response. Cultural interests can bring pleasure. Experiment with a creative project during leisure hours.

May Eve finds a cloud of transits affecting your 6th house. Through the entire month you can be a bit critical and must strive to release stress. The need to serve and contribute is strong. On May 30 Mercury begins a long transit through Cancer; it will quincunx your Sun from the 8th house through August 7. During the summer others will discuss financial needs and ideas. You'll realize how your security is tied to theirs. Discussions about the afterlife or perhaps an inheritance may need attention. Your insight will be extraordinary during this time span. You can get to the bottom of many mysteries. The Full Moon on June 16 is in your sign. This heightens your sensitivity in time for the summer solstice. The lunation accents caring and devotion to ideals as well as individuals. For those who have been searching for a direction, the path becomes clear at this time. July finds Jupiter beginning a year-long transit through Gemini, your opposing sign. In the months to come significant new relationships will develop. Others make plans involving you. Many offers and suggestions are available. Double-check claims and references, though. Be wary of something that seems too good to be true. The triple eclipse pattern in July affects the financial indicators in your birth chart. A new philosophy about values may emerge. New sources of income can be considered by Lammas. During early August Leo transits will affect your 9th house and favorably aspect your Sun. A program of higher education, foreign travel, and meditation sessions can appeal. The last three weeks of August Venus brightens your 10th house. Your charm opens new doors professionally; you will be loved and well-regarded.

September finds Jupiter turning retrograde. This cycle lasts until January 26. It offers a chance to heal old disappointments regarding relationships. A legal question might have to be addressed. Devote the autumnal equinox to rituals blessing your ties to others and to teamwork or harmony.

Halloween should be joyful, for Venus enters your sign several days beforehand. Frolic from mid-October to mid-November. There should be extra money as well as dear ones to share the good times with. Design a Halloween costume to symbolize a favorite romantic hero or heroine. Your 12th house is strong during November. Take time to comfort one who is troubled; a quiet act of kindness brings an unexpected reward. December finds Mercury in your sign. Expect extra travel in the days before Yule. You will express ideas with eloquence and can win the confidence of others.

The eclipses in late December and early January affect finances. Adapt to changing circumstances, develop new salable skills and financial strategies. Recognize what true wealth really is, the value of health and character can seem more precious than gold just now. As Candlemas nears, Aquarius planets affect your 11th house and sextile your Sun. Through early February a new coven or other group can welcome you. Friendships will warm your heart. Choose goals for the future. Mars enters your birth sign on February 15. Through the rest of the winter you will be blessed with a new energy and enthusiasm. Focus on making constructive changes. Much can be accomplished. On March 9, Venus in Aries will turn retrograde in your love sector. You will have a chance to heal old relationships, discover a soul mate from a past life, or understand old patterns regarding others as the year concludes.

HEALTH

The year begins with both Jupiter and Saturn in Taurus in your 6th house of health. The consequences of past health practices, good or bad, will be apparent. Seek healing; develop a fitness regime before Jupiter changes signs in June. A comfortable and healthy work environment is essential this year. Be conscientious about taking good care of yourself. Avoid overwork, exposure to harsh weather, or overly strenuous activities once Mars enters Sagittarius after Valentine's Day.

LOVE

Venus is favorable in April, October 20–November 12, and February 2 through the end of the year. Devote Halloween to the rituals of love; the Goddess should be pleased and reward you with true happiness. It is always easy for you to initiate contact with one whom you admire, for you love the thrill of the chase. Sustaining a relationship through all of its phases is another matter. There is something of the perpetual loner in your nature. Pluto's influence this year encourages depth and intensity. Work at understanding the deeper potentials offered by a worthwhile prospect.

FINANCE

Four of the five eclipses this year affect your financial indicators. There can be a new source of income. Break any negative financial habits; be alert to changes within your business and the economy at large. Values and priorities are shifting. You may redefine wealth. Be very cautious about taking advice from others. Jupiter will oppose your Sun from July on. An offer isn't all it seems to be. After Yule until January 10 Mercury will run rapidly through your 2nd house. That time is favorable for gathering information and making plans to develop solutions to financial situations.

SPIRITUALITY

Neptune's transit this year in your 3rd house hints that magazines and books about spiritual topics can truly inspire you. Visiting different circles and study groups would be worthwhile too. Boredom with the same traditions can make you feel you've reached a spiritual plateau. Examine the mystical teachings of other cultures and adapt them to your own feelings about the sabbats. For example, you might incorporate Mardi Gras traditions at Candlemas or create a basket of decorated eggs for Ostara. Gilded tapers and stained glass lanterns always delight the eye and spirit. Seek new ways to honor the fire elementals for a spiritual lift.

CAPRICORN

*The year ahead for those
born under the sign of the Goat*
December 22–January 20

Goats climb. Your emblem hints that you feel most fulfilled while exploring the top of the mountain. Your standards are high. Still, you are an earth sign and you long for a firm foundation and structure. Capricorns reveal a deliciously dry wit, a subtle and wry humor. This combines in a complex way with a melancholy, gothic nature. You see that we all come into this life alone and leave alone. Still, your sensitive inner psyche so very much wants to be involved in meaningful relationships of all kinds.

Mars crosses the Aries-Taurus cusp with the spring equinox. An unsettled phase regarding home and family life is drawing to a close. You've learned a great deal from taking risks and are now able to integrate the fruits of recent experiences into the quality of your life. March ends with Mars joining the two largest planets, Saturn and Jupiter, in Taurus. This creates a powerful trine to your Sun from the 5th house. The birth of a child is possible. The "baby" could also be a new hobby or creative project. Romance blossoms as the spring flowers open. Life is joyful in late March. April accents fire signs with transits in Aries as well as Sagittarius. Spring fever strikes. Clarify your real yearnings; stick to a schedule. Otherwise you'll drift and dream the month away.

At Beltane, projects begun back in March flower. Supportive influences from Taurus transits bring an impressive creative output. The 5th house is part of this, so expect a memorable romantic interlude that can affect your life for years to come. Late in May, Uranus and Neptune go retrograde in Aquarius. This affects your 2nd house, the money sector. Confusion and changes surrounding income are inevitable. Good or bad, your bank balance isn't what was expected. Be attuned to new trends in your field. This progressive attitude helps financial prospects. You're less materialistic. A free-spirited idealism brushes away the old acquisitiveness.

June 1–17 Venus and the Sun brighten your health sector. It's easier to follow a fitness regime and wholesome diet. Exercise with friends. A shy co-worker expresses interest in friendship. This will take you by surprise, but respond receptively with good grace. Work is a source of greater inspiration and less of a chore. A new animal friend, perhaps a kitten, enters your life just before Midsummer Day. Mars transits your opposing sign of Cancer from mid-June until the eve of Lammas, July 31. You elicit strong reactions under this influence. You certainly won't be ignored, but prepare for enthusiastic approval or adamant rejection. Anticipate many suggestions from others for you are a point of focus, an inspiration, even a role model. Don't let this annoy you near July 16, the date of the eclipse in your birth sign. Just say "no" if concerned about how others are impacting your life. After July 17 communication improves, for Mercury turns direct in your 7th house. As July ends communication is better in regard to relationships. Legal matters can be resolved favorably. Seek expert advice from those who are most experienced.

August finds Saturn, your ruler, entering Gemini where it will remain until mid-October. This affects your 6th house. Take note of health conditions from August to October. Take good care of yourself now to offset any serious conditions in the next few years. Co-workers can be a bit annoying; try not to be too critical of them. A kind offer of help or word of praise will assure good will at work. Saturn is retrograde September 12–January 25. Old cycles are in a finale. You will learn to discard outdated trends and ideas. Near All Hallow's Eve Mars in Virgo will form a trine to Saturn in Taurus. This beautifully highlights your 5th and 9th houses. Expect spiritual insights, meaningful dreams, and meditations. The bright autumn nights crackle with romance. Experiment with creative ideas, for your imagination can lead to an income producing venture.

Mercury retrogrades on the cusp of your 11th house as November begins. News from old friends is likely; you can feel sentimental about an abandoned goal. November 1–7 keep promises and return favors gladly. From early November through Yule, Mars moves through Libra. This affects your 10th house bringing excitement and competition among professional associates. Your career is affected by the way you meet opportunities now. The level of your innate talent and potential is being tested. This can be stressful, but just do the best you can and let the fates guide what happens from there. Changes are in the wind with the winter solstice; December 25 brings a solar eclipse in your birth sign. Adapt to the unexpected. A move or other new opportunity comes near your birthday. The first ten days of January Mercury conjoins your Sun. Travel helps you learn and grow. Dedication and concentration enable you to solve a problem.

Mid-January through Candlemas Venus in Pisces sextiles Saturn. This affects your 3rd house favorably. A neighbor is kind and friendly. Your eloquent communication opens doors. Commuter travel is truly enjoyable. Explore new roads and byways. Share a ride and strengthen a new friendship in the process. From February 2–28 your 2nd house is very active. There is a new market for your skills. Saving to acquire a long-desired purchase brings surprising satisfaction. Financial discussions bring to light new ways to add to your security. Mars slides into your 12th house after Valentine's Day where it will remain through the end of the winter season. An urge to avoid conflict and to act in secret builds. Time spent alone communing with nature or exercising would be rejuvenating. On March 9 Venus turns retrograde in

the home and family sector. Old issues with loved ones can be resolved. Objects which have been missing around the house suddenly reappear. Visitors arrive, and plans to beautify your residence add interest in the days before the spring equinox.

HEALTH
The eclipses in July and December affect you. Be alert to changes within the body. Seek advice and engage in preventative tactics. Focus on creating a healthy work environment. The 6th house is affected by the largest planet, Jupiter, for part of the year. Health improves when Jupiter turns direct on January 26.

LOVE
A new relationship is likely for there are two eclipses in your 7th house of marriage. July 1 and January 9 are the pivotal dates. Be receptive to new ideas a partner voices then. Saturn is in your 5th house most of the year. An attraction to a stable, nurturing partner with experience grows.

FINANCE
Wildly unpredictable times are to be expected regarding security. Electrical Uranus and mystical Neptune are in your money sector. Your attitude toward money is going through a transformation. Metaphysical and artistic aptitudes can lead you into a new profession. There can be a roller coaster ride of highs and lows charting your income. Avoid tying up funds. Keep extra cash available.

SPIRITUALITY
Changes in the status quo this year will provide a new perspective on the true meaning of your life. The eclipse pattern in Capricorn promises this. Spiritual awakenings can occur near July 16 and again January 9. Take time to meditate and reflect on those dates.

AQUARIUS

*The year ahead for those
born under the sign of the Water Bearer*
January 21–February 19

The idealistic reformer of the zodiac, you are full of contradictions. New ideas appeal and you have an intellectual temperament, yet you seldom allow external influences to change your life in any way. Television and the theater attract you, for they can provide an uninvolved, detached release for deepest feelings. Comfortable friendship provides an easier way for you to relate to others than an excess of emotions or passions. Your emblem, the Water Bearer, pours out the water of life on barren ground. This hints that your mission is to facilitate growth for a bright new future.

Uranus, your ruler, and Neptune both transit your birth sign throughout the year. You are in the midst of a personal odyssey of discovery and transition. New people and interests enter your life. Your sensitivity is heightened; learn to trust your intuition. With the vernal equinox your 2nd house is accented by Pisces planets. Money will be the prime concern through April 9. Your creativity or contact with a sympathetic friend can aid earning ability. From March 23 until just after May Eve Mars will affect your home and family sector. Your home might need extra maintenance. A relative can be rather volatile. Devote May Day rituals to a blessing on the family and protection for the residence. From May through the summer solstice Gemini transits harmonize with you. The 5th house is affected. Romantic interludes bring delight. A new avocation captures your inter-

est and might put you in touch with a whole new group of people. It's a marvelous time to plan special journeys.

On June 24 Mercury turns retrograde in the 6th house where it will aspect the Sun, Mars, and Venus through mid-July. Focus on well-being. Alternative health practices can help. Information comes to light which changes old perceptions about co-workers. A special animal friend shows tremendous rapport. Jupiter enters your 5th house June 30 where it will remain through the end of the year. For those who long to have a child, that wish can be fulfilled. A love affair leads to growth and new happiness. Aquarian artists and entertainers will begin a very productive year. On July 30 the solar eclipse affects partnerships. A commitment can end or begin near that day; closest bonds are in a state of flux. At Lammastide the Sun, Venus, and Mars gather together in your opposing sign of Leo. As the month moves along it will be essential to look at both sides of every issue. Negotiate. Others involve you in plans. Teamwork enables you to accomplish much. When Saturn enters Gemini on August 10 you will feel a lessening of the ongoing responsibility and stress you've had to endure related to home and family life. The Full Moon in Aquarius on August 15 sheds light on the application of your talents. Throughout the rest of the month doors will open; prepare to demonstrate your best efforts.

Venus crosses into Libra at the start of September. This creates a lovely trine to your Sun from the 9th house which stays in force until September 24. The entire month brings a unique eloquence and beauty to your words. Speak to groups or write; you can uplift others. A deep philosophical and spiritual quality comes into love relationships. A friend from another land or different socioeconomic background can become very close. After the autumn equinox passes and cosmic energies gather near your midheaven, your career goals will become more ambitious. Your charm and quick wits will impress the influential during the first half of October. You will be more competitive than usual as Halloween nears, for on October 16 Saturn retrogrades into

Taurus where it will remain at a square to your Sun for the rest of the year. This will serve as a motivating influence. The stress level can be rather high, but you can accomplish much through persistent, patient effort. The Full Moon in Taurus on November 11 will bring the specifics to light. Be diplomatic November 9–December 3, for Mercury makes a difficult aspect. If uncertain about speaking out, sending a letter, or making a call, don't do it. It's better to say too little than too much. Yuletide should be a joyful time, with many opportunities to celebrate, for Venus is in your sign from early December through January 3. Pursue financial opportunities then too.

The eclipses of December and January affect your 6th and 12th houses. Be alert to health conditions; pay extra attention to the well-being of animals also. You might enjoy being alone during mid-January, reveling in peace and privacy. From January 10 until Candlemas Mercury is in Aquarius. You'll be able to make the best choices and express yourself well. Pursue opportunities for study and travel. February 7 Mercury retrogrades into Aquarius where it will remain until March 17. This marvelous mobility and mental clarity will return with even greater impact at that time. Venus will brighten your 3rd house from early February through winter's end. Short journeys will delight you. A neighbor or sibling expresses affection and admiration. You would enjoy the study of art and music. After February 15 Mars will be in Sagittarius sextile your Sun. This encourages new plans and gives healing energy. A health problem or bad experience is overcome and you feel better than ever with the approach of spring.

HEALTH

The eclipses on July 1 and January 9 profoundly affect your health, for they fall in your 6th house. Be alert to changing health conditions and seek advice. Try different health care techniques if one isn't working. You are very sensitive to temperature extremes, especially the cold. Protect yourself from them. Health trends look bright as the year ends and any problems should fade away February–March.

LOVE

September and December Venus will be in harmonious aspect. Romance can bloom then, or a present attachment may deepen. November 4–December 23 passionate Mars will be in your 5th house. This could bring a new fire to your love life. You can experience especially deep feelings. Plan a love tryst near Yule. Friendship is an indispensable part of love for you. You will often begin a relationship with that in mind and the romance follows. Be certain that you enjoy each other's mutual circles of friends when contemplating a serious commitment.

FINANCE

Benevolent Jupiter will enter your brother air sign of Gemini at the close of June and will trine your Sun. A cycle of growth and prosperity is promised during the rest of the year. At the same time Saturn in Taurus in your 4th house could make family obligations or housing costs affect your financial picture. Uranus, your ruler, turns direct October 27, following a long retrograde. After that it will be easier to break old patterns and to move forward from then on. The secret to moving forward this year financially might lie in keeping the overhead low.

SPIRITUALITY

Neptune is in the midst of a long transit through your birth sign. The material world can seem almost foreign. Spiritual values are becoming more important than ever. You will draw away from the mechanics of ritual and dwell on spiritual awakening coming through dreams or meditations. A new sense of aliens, angels, or other entities being nearby will be strong.

PISCES

The year ahead for those
born under the sign of the Fish
February 20–March 20

Your world revolves around feelings and dreams. With your vivid imagination, finding a positive creative outlet is a must. You reflect the moods of the people and places around you, just as a still pond mirrors the sky. You have a deep compassion toward all who suffer, including animals. Charity work is deeply fulfilling. You express a hospitality that disarms any adversaries. Use subtle strategy, for you are adept at achieving desired results before opponents realize what's happening.

Spring drifts in with a sweetness. Venus is in your birth sign at the vernal equinox and remains there until April 6. Express feelings of love; experiment with creative ideas. Add color and beauty to yourself and your surroundings. All year Pluto will square your Sun while remaining in your 10th house. Expect power struggles at work; questions of credibility must be resolved. One stage of your professional life might end and a new one begin. Mars will favorably accent your 3rd house from early spring through May Eve. Extra commuter travel is likely; prepare for an abundance of calls and letters. Purchasing a new vehicle or securing travel tickets is likely. On May 9 Neptune, your ruler, begins a long retrograde. Dreams and meditations take a nostalgic turn. Learn from old habits and patterns. Make the most of time spent alone in the weeks to come, for your 12th house is highlighted. During the last half of May Mercury will square your Sun while moving rapidly through your 4th house. Unexpected visitors will enliven the household, but relatives can be a little noisy and restless. There can be plans to move or redecorate. During June several planets move into your pleasure and romance sector. A new hobby sparks enthusiasm. You can travel with or learn from a lover near Midsummer Eve.

July's three eclipses will activate your 5th, 11th, and 6th houses. Your goals are changing. New friendships develop and old ties loosen. Love has an element of surprise. Be flexible with upheavals in your daily schedule. Look upon adjustments as catalysts for growth. Your health care and fitness regimes may require attention. After Lammastide Saturn crosses the Taurus-Gemini cusp and will join Jupiter in your 4th house. Balance the urge to find a more spacious and comfortable home with practical considerations. Family members are going through some growth and changes. New insights about heritage and the family tree can come to light. Late August through September 7 Mercury will oppose your Sun. Listen to the ideas and advice of others. Learn from a companion. The Full Moon in Pisces September 13 aspects Pluto. There can be contact with spirit beings and angels that night. A phase of your professional life is about to end. Look upon this as a chance to develop new opportunities. After the autumn equinox Venus enters Scorpio and will trine your Sun until October 19. Foreign-born friends will be congenial. Travels will be a source of inspiration and delight. Try your hand at penning a sonnet or short story.

Neptune turns direct October 16. A sense of purpose develops by All Hallows' Eve. You will progress. Take note of creative inspirations and intuitive flashes. Mercury will trine your Sun during November, involving the 9th house. Students absorb knowledge readily; it's a perfect time to enroll in classes. Philosophy and history discussions can be a source of stimulating new ideas. Make decisions after November 8 when Mercury completes its retrograde. As December opens, Mars in Libra is quincunx your Sun and agitating the 8th house. Don't be tempted to betray a confidence. Avoid getting into financial entanglements with others. Keep your own counsel, for power shared is power lost. Secrecy and discretion are followed by the wise.

After Yule, Mars enters Scorpio where it will radiate strength and warmth in your life through Valentine's Day. The dark, cold winter days find you glowing with new ideas and enthusiasm. The eclipses on December 25 and January 9 promise new relationships and recreations. A friend can change the course of your life. Venus transits your sign from January 4 through Candlemas. Be receptive and responsive, for you have admirers who would express love if encouraged. Make special efforts with your appearance. Clothing and adornments chosen now will amplify your desirability. February accents Aquarius planets in your 12th house. You will have an active inner life; your depth and subtlety will intrigue others. You are an enigma without intending to be. During March mutable aspects are strong, especially in the case of Mars square your Sun. Competitive feelings develop. A desire for advancement and recognition at work may become a focus. Much is expected of you. Music and humor can help you control stress. March 9 finds Venus turning retrograde in your 2nd house. Reconsider the purchase of luxury items. It might be wisest to save and budget. Expensive gifts which are either received or given might have strings attached. Loved ones voice a need to feel more secure.

HEALTH
Summer is the most important time for health care this year, for the eclipse on July 30 in Leo falls in your 6th house. Be aware of changing health needs. Resolve to form good habits. Get plenty of cardiovascular exercise. Purchase a juicer and add fresh fruit and vegetables to your diet. The Sun's healing power can work wonders this year. While avoiding the harsh glare of midday, do spend plenty of time in the full-spectrum outdoor light near dusk or dawn. Try deep breathing exercises to heal and balance from within.

LOVE
Venus begins the year with a transit through your birth sign. Spring is the season of love and will be a theme which holds true this year. The eclipses of July 1 and January 9 both affect your 5th house, the love sector. You can have several changes of heart. Existing relationships unfold in a new direction. It's a year of discovery regarding love and pleasure. Try to clarify your definition of what love truly is. Times of great bliss followed by turmoil and more bliss are certain. Be patient regarding any new commitments.

FINANCE
During April you will talk and think a great deal about money, for Mercury will transit your 2nd house. You might accept a second job or decide to learn a new salable skill then. From the vernal equinox until June 30 benevolent Jupiter makes a lucky sextile to your Sun. Follow through with opportunities which materialize then, for wise decisions and investments can create good fortune through the rest of the year. Devote the summer solstice to prosperity magic and affirmations. Later in the year Jupiter and Saturn will transit Gemini and create a reckless square to your Sun. This can bring expenses related to home and family needs. Resist the temptation to take risks, for they can lead to a disappointment by Yule.

SPIRITUALITY
Uranus and Neptune in Aquarius will span your 12th house all year. The spirit of sacrifice and charity will move you. Doing quiet good deeds for those in need can bring a deep happiness. Discover the spiritual truths in nature. Meditation in a wilderness area can lead to attunement with higher forces. Visit places of unusual natural beauty such as national parks.

Arthur Rackham

SEVEN AGES OF MAN

All the world's a stage,
And all the men and women merely players:
They have their exits and their entrances;
And one man in his time plays many parts,
His acts being seven ages. As, first the infant,
Mewling and puking in the nurse's arms.
And then the whining schoolboy, with his satchel
And shining morning face, creeping like snail
Unwillingly to school. And then the lover,
Sighing like furnace, with a woeful ballad
Made to his mistress' eyebrow. Then the soldier,
Full of strange oaths, and bearded like the pard,
Jealous in honour, sudden and quick in quarrel,
Seeking the bubble reputation
Even in the cannon's mouth. And then the justice,
In fair round belly with good capon lined,
With eyes severe and beard of formal cut,
Full of wise saws and modern instances;
And so he plays his part. The sixth age shifts
Into the lean and slipper'd pantaloon,
With spectacles on nose and pouch on side;
His youthful hose, well saved, a world too wide
For his shrunk shank; and his big manly voice,
Turning again toward childish treble, pipes
And whistles in his sound. Last scene of all,
That ends this strange eventful history,
Is second childishness and mere oblivion,
Sans teeth, sans eyes, sans taste, sans everything.

— SHAKESPEARE
As You Like It

THE CELTIC TREE CALENDAR

Beth (Birch)	December 24 to January 20
Luis (Rowan)	January 21 to February 17
Nion (Ash)	February 18 to March 17
Fearn (Alder)	March 18 to April 14
Saille (Willow)	April 15 to May 12
Uath (Hawthorn)	May 13 to June 9
Duir (Oak)	June 10 to July 7
Tinne (Holly)	July 8 to August 4
Coll (Hazel)	August 5 to September 1
Muin (Vine)	September 2 to September 29
Gort (Ivy)	September 30 to October 27
Ngetal (Reed)	October 28 to November 24
Ruis (Elder)	November 25 to December 22

December 23 is not ruled by any tree for it is the "day" of the proverbial "year and day" in the earliest courts of law.

THE WAY OF THE MOON

A New Moon rises with the Sun,
Her waxing half at midday shows,
The Full Moon climbs at sunset hour,
And waning half the midnight knows.

NEW	2001	FULL	NEW	2002	FULL
January 24		January 9	January 13		January 28
February 23		February 8	February 12		February 27
March 24		March 9	March 13		March 28
April 23		April 7	April 12		April 26
May 22		May 7	May 12		May 26
June 21		June 5	June 10		June 24
July 20		July 5	July 10		July 24
August 18		August 4	August 8		August 22
September 17		September 2	September 6		September 21
October 16		October 2	October 6		October 21
November 15		November 1/30	November 4		November 19
December 14		December 30	December 4		December 19

Life takes on added dimension when you match your activities to the waxing and waning of the Moon. Observe the sequence of her phases to learn the wisdom of constant change within complete certainty.

THE WITCHES' QUARTERLY

This quarterly newsletter appears at each change of season: the vernal equinox (March 21st), summer solstice (June 21st), the autumnal equinox (September 21st), and winter solstice (December 21st). Each issue boasts a myriad of special features including an astrological forecast for each day, myths, useful information about plants and animals, and rituals and lore to help celebrate the passing seasons. Available by subscription. 12 pages. Mailed in a discreet envelope.

Subscription rates:

1/2 year (two seasons)	$16.00
1 year (four seasons)	$28.00

To order: Send your name and address along with a check or money order payable in U.S. funds to: Witchery Company, PO Box 4067, Middletown, RI, 02842

...other titles *from The Witches' Almanac*

ANCIENT ROMAN HOLIDAYS

The glory that was Rome awaits you in Barbara Stacy's classic presentation of a festive year in pagan times. From Janus, god of beginnings, to Saturn's wintery feast, the text is complemented with illustrations by 19th-century antiquarian Thomas Hope drawn from archaic sources. Here are the gods and goddesses as the Romans conceived them, accompanied by the annual rites performed in their worship. Scholarly, lighthearted—a rare combination. 64 pages.

LOVE FEASTS

Creating meals to share with the one you love can be a sacred ceremony in itself. With the witch in mind, culinary adept Christine Fox offers magical menus and recipes for every month in the year.

For ordering information, turn the page.

MOON LORE

As both the largest and the brightest object in the night sky, and the only one to appear in phases, the Moon has been a rich source of myth for as long as there have been myth-makers.

Elizabeth Pepper's *Moon Lore* is a compendium of lunar tales, charms, chants, and curses from ancient time to the present.

A BOOK OF DAYS

A delightful book for friends of all ages. Here are 1700 gemlike quotations dealing with all aspects of human life, drawn from every source imaginable—from earliest records to the present, from Aristotle to Thurber. Quotations begin with Spring and Youth, then to Summer and Maturity, on to Autumn and Harvest, then Winter and Rest. Illustrated with over 200 medieval woodcuts.

RANDOM RECOLLECTIONS Vol's. I, II, III, IV.

Pages culled from the original (no longer available) issues of *The Witches' Almanac,* published annually throughout the 1970's, are now available in a series of tasteful booklets. A treasure for those who missed us the first time around; keepsakes for those who remember.

CELTIC TREE MAGIC

Robert Graves in *The White Goddess* writes of the significance of trees in the old Celtic lore. *Celtic Tree Magic* is an investigation of the sacred trees in the remarkable Beth-Luis-Nion alphabet; their role in folklore, poetry, and mysticism. Richly illustrated as you've come to expect from our publications.

LOVE CHARMS

Love has many forms, many aspects. Ceremonies performed in witchcraft celebrate the joy and the blessings of love. This is the theme of Elizabeth Pepper's *Love Charms.* It's a collection of love charms to use now and ever after.

Order Form

Each edition of *The Witches' Almanac* is a unique journey through the classic stylings of Elizabeth Pepper and John Wilcock. Limited numbers of previous years' editions are available.

_____2000 - 2001 The Witches' Almanac @ $7.95_____

_____1999 - 2000 The Witches' Almanac @ $7.95_____

_____1998 - 1999 The Witches' Almanac @ $6.95_____

_____1997 - 1998 The Witches' Almanac @ $6.95_____

_____1996 - 1997 The Witches' Almanac @ $6.95_____

_____1995 - 1996 The Witches' Almanac @ $6.95_____

_____1994 - 1995 The Witches' Almanac @ $5.95_____

_____1993 - 1994 The Witches' Almanac @ $5.95_____

_____Celtic Tree Magic @ $6.95_____

_____Love Charms @ $5.95_____

_____Random Recollection I @ $3.95_____

_____Random Recollection II @ $3.95_____

_____Random Recollection III @ $3.95_____

_____Random Recollection IV @ $3.95_____

_____A Book of Days @ $15.95_____

_____Moon Lore @ $6.95_____

_____Love Feasts @ $6.95_____

_____Ancient Roman Holidays @ $6.95_____

_____Magic Charms from A to Z @ $12.95_____

Shipping and handling charges:
One book: $2.50 — each additional book, add $1.00

Send your name and address along with a check or money order payable in U. S. funds to:
The Witches' Almanac
Mail Order Dept.,
PO Box 4067, Middletown, R I 02842

*Subtotal*_____

*Shipping & handling*_____

*Sales tax (RI orders only)*_____

*Total*_____

A CATALOG

A collection of hard-to-find quality items sure to be of interest
to the serious practitioner. To obtain your copy of this full-color
catalog, send $2 along with your name and address to:

Witchery
Post Office Box 4067
Middletown, Rhode Island, 02842

TO: The Witches' Almanac, P.O. Box 4067, Middletown, RI, 02842

Name _____

Address _____

City _____ State _____ Zip _____

WITCHCRAFT being by nature one of
the secretive arts it may not be as easy
to find us next year. If you'd like to
make sure we know where *you* are, why
don't you send us your name & address? You'll certainly hear from us.